Uncommon Practice

People who deliver a great brand experience

Compliments of

Jim Thacher

The Forum Corporation
www.forum.com

Interbrand   FORUM®

Prentice Hall

FINANCIAL TIMES

London • New York • San Francisco • Toronto • Sydney
Tokyo • Singapore • Hong Kong • Cape Town • Madrid
Paris • Milan • Munich • Amsterdam

In an increasingly competitive world, we believe it's quality of
thinking that will give you the edge – an idea that opens new
doors, a technique that solves a problem, or an insight that
simply makes sense of it all. The more you know, the smarter
and faster you can go.

That's why we work with the best minds in business and finance
to bring cutting-edge thinking and best learning practice to a
global market.

Under a range of leading imprints, including Financial Times
Prentice Hall, we create world-class print publications and
electronic products bringing our readers knowledge, skills and
understanding which can be applied whether studying or at work.

To find out more about our business publications, or tell us about
the books you'd like to find, you can visit us at www.business-
minds.com

For other Pearson Education publications, visit
www.pearsoned-ema.com

Pearson
Education

About Interbrand and Forum

Interbrand

Founded in 1974, the Interbrand group is the world's leading brand consultancy. Interbrand's services and people are dedicated to creating, developing and managing clients' most valuable assets – their brands. The company has worked with over 70 of the Fortune 100 companies through disciplines including strategic consultancy, corporate and brand identity, brand valuation, research, name development, internal brand management, digital branding, tone of voice and trademark law. Interbrand's people are recruited worldwide from a variety of backgrounds, from accountancy to design and from management consultancy to multimedia production. Interbrand has published a succession of books on brand-related subjects including *The Future of Brands* (Palgrave, 2000) and top-selling business book *We, Me, Them & It* (Texere, 2000). To find out more about Interbrand, please visit us at www.interbrand.com

Forum, an FT Knowledge company, is a global workplace-learning corporation that helps large, leading businesses create learning strategies, develop learning solutions, manage their learning organizations and deploy their brands. Its clients include more than 130 members of the Fortune 500. For three decades, Forum has helped companies improve leadership, management, team building, sales, sales management and service excellence. It is the largest provider in the world of outsourced training management services. Through its Customer Experience service, Forum helps businesses turn their brand promises into employee behaviours and processes that create lasting customer loyalty. For more information on creating a Customer Experience, visit us at www.forum.com

PEARSON EDUCATION LIMITED

Head Office:
Edinburgh Gate
Harlow CM20 2JE
Tel: +44 (0)1279 623623
Fax: +44 (0)1279 431059

London Office:
128 Long Acre
London WC2E 9AN
Tel: +44 (0)20 7447 2000
Fax: +44 (0)20 7240 5771
Website: www.business-minds.com

First published in Great Britain in 2002

© Pearson Education Limited 2002

The right of Interbrand Newell & Sorrell and Forum to be identified as
Authors of this work has been asserted by them in accordance
with the Copyright, Designs and Patents Act 1988.

ISBN 0 273 65936 7

British Library Cataloguing in Publication Data
A CIP catalogue record for this book can be obtained from the British Library.

10 9 8 7 6 5

Typeset by Pantek Arts Ltd, Maidstone, Kent.
Printed and bound by Rotolito Lombarda, Italy.
Illustrations by Ben Kirchner © Ben Kirchner
Ben Kirchner represented by Heart UK

The Publishers' policy is to use paper manufactured from sustainable forests.

Contents

"This book takes an original approach to its subject and comes up with some uncommonly useful lessons."

Rufus Olins, editor-in-chief and publisher, *Management Today*

"This is a terrific book. It paints a picture of what the 21st Century company has to look like ... This is not about clever advertising but creating a genuine commitment among employees to provide customers with a unique, quality experience.

What makes the book different is that the authors have chosen 19 fascinating businesses... they let the top executives do the talking about what makes their companies different. It provides a host of up-to-date insights for managers and MBAs."

Professor Peter Doyle, Warwick Business School

"How often do you get the chance to have an unmediated head-to-head with business leaders who are delivering on the new frontier of business – the customer experience?

If you want to hear direct from Richard Branson and his lieutenants, Carphone Warehouse's Charles Dunstone and other uncommon business leaders – many of whom are notoriously reluctant to be interviewed – *Uncommon Practice* is the book that lets you hear their story straight from the horse's mouth."

Phil Dourado, Editorial Director, eCustomerServiceWorld.com

Thank You

There are a number of people whom we would like to thank because without them this book would not have seen the light of day. In particular, we would like to thank Alison Rawlinson, Carmelita Lubos, Diane Woodworth-Jordan and Saskia Diemer who helped to identify the companies featured in this book, conducted key research and some of the interviews; they also worked tirelessly to co-ordinate the interviews and ensure all transcripts were approved. We would also like to thank Rachel Woolf who with her usual good humour and grace, transcribed all the interviews at an amazing rate and with extraordinary accuracy. Andrea Letica who had the idea of the striking and original design approach for the book, Ben Kirchner whose illustrations grace the pages and Giuseppe Preti who diligently produced the artwork. They worked with professionalism and a great deal of grace under the pressure of changing briefs and shortening deadlines. To our colleagues who conducted many of the interviews and gave their expert opinions on what was unique about the companies: Tom Blackett, Iain Carruthers, Tom Knighton, Ronan Knox, Wayne Marks, David Simmons, Stacey Hatcher, Scott Timmins, Bill Fonvielle, Diann Strausberg, Sarah McIntosh, Bill Ghormley, Bill Woolfolk, Ken Brown and Peter Pickus.

Thanks also to Caroline Wilson, veteran of many a book, for providing a firm, challenging and expert editorial viewpoint, to Jackie Draper, Jennifer Wolf, Tracey Richardson and Jane Kennedy for their support in the efforts to promote the book. To the team at FTPH, Richard Stagg and especially Sarah Harper, for their expert advice and patience in the long process of preparing this book. To Anne Lockhart who juggled diaries to ensure we managed to meet once in a while.

Special thanks to Rita Clifton who not only conducted interviews and helped formulate our approach but most importantly supported this book and the people responsible for it with passion and conviction.

Finally, a very special thank you to Catriona Crombie who took on the enormous challenge of ensuring that the book moved from its conception to its delivery to the publishers. Her dedication, attention to detail and good humour through all the changes and difficulties in assembling this book impressed everyone who worked with her and have earned her the undying gratitude of us all. She demonstrated an uncommon practice which would have deserved a chapter of its own!

Andy Milligan and Shaun Smith
Spring 2002

Introduction

What do we mean by uncommon practice?

There are some companies we look at and think 'they really do it differently, don't they?' We may not necessarily be customers of theirs, we might not even be customers they would target; yet we admire them, even if it might be grudgingly, because they clearly deliver what they promise and that is the essence of great brand building.

The premise behind this book is that such companies succeed because their cultures are uniquely developed to meet the needs of their customers in a distinctive way. Critical to the development of that culture is a genuine belief in, and commitment to, the people in the business that has engendered a loyalty uncommon amongst many organizations. This loyalty translates into a genuine passion for their customers.

This book is called *Uncommon Practice* because we believe that this approach to business is not the norm. These uncommon companies often do things that are unusual, ground-breaking and which defy conventional business wisdom, 'daring to be daft', to paraphrase Richard Branson.

In order to test whether that uniqueness is genuine, we decided to let the people who created or are creating those cultures do the talking. To record in their own words what they think about the places in which they work. To hear them literally 'talk the walk', rather than to provide an editorial gloss over their words. This means that from chapter to chapter we hear the different tones in which that culture speaks, from the passionate entrepreneurialism of Pret A Manger, to the enthusiasm and energy that is Harley-Davidson, to the fun and irreverence of Virgin, to the measured, consultative tones of John Lewis. For it is the way that they speak and the words that they use that help to mark out these businesses as 'uncommon'.

What is the purpose of this book?

This is a book which is intended to give insights into how certain companies provide such remarkable experiences and prove to be successful at doing it too. The book is intended to appeal to everyone from the general reader, who is interested in knowing what the people behind the brands he or she often experiences actually think, to the CEO looking for some insight or inspiration to help him or her create a more dynamic business. Above all, it is essential for everyone who believes that great brands are built on a genuine commitment by their owners to deliver something valuable to customers which nobody else can provide. Furthermore, this book should provide plenty of evidence for those who believe that by creating something that has genuine meaning for customers, people can find genuine meaning in their jobs.

This book is not a 'how to...' book, it is not intended to distil the wide variety of different companies and experiences (in different sectors, markets, geographies) into a 'quick-fix' list of invariable rules for success. Nevertheless, we have abstracted certain core principles and practices that these companies share but seem to us to be uncommon, generally, in business. We share our findings and interpretations in the conclusion.

We are also sure that many of the situations and observations of the interviewees will strike a familiar chord with people. The most important one being: 'how do I motivate and retain the people who work for me while creating a successful business that customers value?' Not surprisingly, the answer on which all our interviewees agree is that by looking after your own people, you take best care of your customers.

How did we choose the companies in this book?

Consultants from Interbrand and Forum offices in the UK and USA were asked to nominate companies which they thought:

- had a very distinctive brand proposition
- delivered this proposition to customers consistently
- had a reputation for loyal staff
- had enthusiastic customers
- were successful.

We were also keen to include companies which had not been 'done to death' in textbooks and case studies. So although well known established brands such as Virgin and Tesco are included, we have also included brands whose stories might not be so familiar such as Richer Sounds, Krispy Kreme, Harrah's and Carphone Warehouse, as well as organizations which might not be regarded classically as brands, such as Oxfam.

We then interviewed key executives of the companies to discover:

- what they thought their brands stand for
- how the brand affected their operations, particularly the delivery of the customer experience
- what the role of their people was in developing this
- how they created and maintained a distinctive culture.

The people interviewed, in the main, were responsible for:

- strategy and leadership (usually the CEO but not always)
- human resources (usually the HR Director but not always)
- marketing (usually the Marketing Director but not always)
- operations/customer service (usually the Operations/Customer Services Director but not always).

In fact, one of the interesting features of the companies is that most of them do not see these functions as being the sole responsibility of key individuals. What seems to unite these companies is the belief that the customer experience is what matters and that HR, operations, strategy and marketing are interdependent in delivering that experience.

For Oxfam and Manchester United, we also interviewed people who are volunteers or former players in order to reflect the special nature of those organizations.

In approaching these companies there were certain myths and preconceptions that pervade businesses today which we were interested in exploring. These include:

- Should you assume that the customer is always right?
- Who should come first, your people or your customers?
- Is a focus on the bottom line the main driver of financial success?
- Are external communications more important than internal communications?
- Is harmonizing the culture the first step following a merger?
- Which is more important: hiring right or training right?
- Is advertising and promotion the fastest way to build a brand?
- Is investing in the 'soft stuff' a waste of time?
- Is it true that you should hire the best MBAs you can find?
- Is walking the talk an overused cliché?

You can judge for yourself what you think the answers to these questions are – we summarize our conclusions at the end of the book.

Why do we think a book like this is important?

We have long argued that the value of brands to businesses is that they represent a reliable and protectable stream of ongoing revenues. Interbrand has also been able to identify and quantify that value economically to the satisfaction of organizations like the New York and London stock exchanges and tax authorities. However, this focus on the economic value of brands has sometimes distracted attention from an appreciation of their organizational value. By which we mean that organizations can create value in a number of ways for their various stakeholders by having a differentiated customer-focused idea and a way of doing things which is unique.

By focusing on creating something meaningful and relevant for customers, and doing so in a way that is clearly differentiated from others, these organizations create meaning and relevance for their employees. And for a PLC, as Terry Leahy points out in his interview, that is how you create value for your shareholders too. What we mean by brand, therefore, is not the artificial projection of an image protected by a trademark, but the genuine delivery of a unique experience promised by a brand name.

There are also insights in these interviews into the increasing importance of fun in the workplace, of empowering employees to take decisions, of being 'intimate' with your customers even when you are the chief executive (in fact, especially when you are the CEO) and, above all, of a fine old-fashioned value that is, we hope, being rediscovered in business: 'integrity' in your relationships not only with customers and employees but also with suppliers and shareholders.

The success of the companies in this book is measured in many ways: by customer satisfaction, employee satisfaction, good profits, high revenues, even esteem amongst peers (it is interesting to note how often the interviewees refer to other brands featured in the book). What they all have in common, and this is uncommon, is that bottom line figures alone are not enough to judge the success of a business. They all appreciate that 'lead' measures, ie, those measures which predict customer behaviour – such as customer satisfaction, employee satisfaction, brand equity – are as important as the 'lag' measures that have told you how well you have done. And they constantly review their results.

Finally, a note on how to read this book

We have made our own conclusions about these companies and abstracted some common themes and some tips. However, what is more important is that you as a reader decide on what seems relevant and important. You can gain insights from reading just one chapter or you can compare the themes and differences that make these organizations similar but unique. Above all, draw your own conclusions. In encouraging you to do this, rather than prescribe a recipe for you, we hope we are ourselves showing an uncommon practice. We believe that cook books and management books belong on different shelves.

Andy Milligan **Interbrand**   Shaun Smith **Forum**

Virgin

1

Virgin probably remains most people's idea of the maverick, customer-focused brand. From its beginnings as a record store to its recent highly successful venture into financial services, Virgin has prided itself on challenging industry norms to deliver a better experience and better value for customers.

Virgin Atlantic summarizes this approach with its distinctive, fun and irreverent approach; it has won numerous awards over the years for the quality of its customer service and has pioneered many innovations in customer service. Virgin's decision to take on one of the rail franchises in the UK is another example of its desire to transform perceptions of a particular industry, however difficult that might be.

The personality of Richard Branson has been deliberately promoted to provide a transparent, public face for the organization, but as these interviews demonstrate, the challenging, fun and irreverent culture of the brand runs deeper than one man.

1

Richard Branson

Chairman

I was jumping on and off planes and I couldn't find one positive redeeming factor about any of the airlines I flew on. I felt we could set up an airline that treated people as human beings and was a pleasure to fly rather than one that everyone had to grin and bear. Virgin Atlantic was born with one aeroplane. One of the advantages we had was that we could take on 150 people who had the right attitude: outward-going, friendly, smiling, who cared about other people. They weren't necessarily people who had flown on other airlines before so they hadn't felt that they'd seen it all before and got bored with it all. They had a freshness about them, they came with lots of new ideas, and they came with the attitude of 'just because it hadn't been done before it didn't mean we couldn't do it'. In every area of the plane, whether it was first class, business class or economy class, new ideas were brought to bear and the idea was to try and create the best airline in the world – not the biggest – and make sure that, year after year, our staff was voted the best.

Anytime I'm on a plane I try to make sure that I'm not sleeping the whole way; that I get out and about and talk to everybody. I always have a notebook on me, I don't just talk to my staff about ideas for service but also ideas for improvements for them personally. I come back with 20 to 25 little suggestions: whether it's 'the blouse is too thin', 'the shoes are uncomfortable', 'I'd love to have some unpaid leave'; just lots and lots of things that will make their jobs more pleasant.

I write to them every couple of months, the last paragraph of my letter is always 'if you have any ideas or suggestions, this is my home address, please write'. It might take a month for me to get back to everybody, but they know that letters from staff take priority over letters from everybody else. So we get about 20 letters a day from staff and not just from airline staff or train staff but all across the company. Once a year we have a staff party where everybody gets together. There are so many people working for Virgin that the parties last for six days, they have it in my home in the country and the last one we had was for about 70,000 people. I try to make sure that I shake hands with everyone as they arrive and then try to get out and about and party and mix as much as possible – by the end of the week I need a new body! When we took over a big chunk of British Rail, the staff had just never been to anything like that before and it was a tremendous morale booster to have them come to my home and be treated properly.

We get an enormous amount of letters every day. Any letter from staff members I read myself. For instance, if somebody is getting married and needs an extra week off. You might say they should go to their managers, but sometimes it's out of frustration that maybe someone has been to the people who are looking after them and have found they haven't been able to get everything they want so they come to me direct. More often than not I'll cut through the issue and they're given what they want. My philosophy is to look for the best in people, give them the benefit of the doubt and you get the best in return. If you give people a lot of trust and praise, people give their all back. If I give a

'Uncommon Practice' at Virgin

Annual garden party for 30,000 staff plus their partners and families

Profit share scheme

Customer-service group to spread best practice

'Back to the floor' programme at Virgin Atlantic

Tribe employee-discount scheme

Great Service Awards scheme at Virgin Trains

Open management and open door policy

Virgin Charter across the group linked to brand standards

Employee holidays on Necker Island

steward a year off to learn to become a pilot, he will come back and be extremely grateful and give his all. Obviously you can't sort out everybody's problem, but we can try and sort out 90 percent of them. I've always said I would put my people first, customers second and shareholders third, but the truth of the matter is if you do that, the customers and the shareholders benefit anyway.

I wouldn't necessarily say that Virgin people are radically different from other people in other companies. I think the difference is that in most Virgin companies the companies are small and we're striving to make sure the quality of the company is the best in its field and therefore the staff are proud that they work for Virgin. When they talk to their friends in the evening or at the pub and they say 'I work for Virgin' they're proud of that fact. We spend a lot more money trying to get every little detail right so that when our staff come to work they know they're working for the best company in their particular field. I suspect there are other people in other companies that are just as good, it's just that they're not as proud. Somebody working for another airline might find that the quality of the goods that they're given to work with, the state of the aeroplanes, the state of the seats, etc, is not that great and therefore it's difficult to feel motivated and proud of what you're doing. This is true also if you're part of an enormous conglomerate where nobody seems to care or listen. The reason people leave companies is not generally due to lack of pay: it's due to not being proud of the company they're working for and not being listened to. So we've always got to fight against the danger of our getting too big by making sure that we keep our companies in small units and that we've got people listening all the time.

I spend very little time in the office; 250 days a year I'm travelling outside the country visiting our foreign companies and a lot of the time is spent on Virgin planes. I try to be out and about meeting people as much as possible. I've just come back from Australia where I spent a week there and every night we had a party. We had a party to celebrate the first anniversary of Virgin Blue; we had a party to celebrate the first anniversary of Virgin Mobiles in Australia, and then every other city that we went to we had a party for those people who couldn't make the other parties. On top of that we were offered a quarter of a billion dollars to sell out Virgin Blue; we'd only been going a year. I just felt that it was tempting but we would've sold out our people there.

We're tearing the airline industry apart in Australia; we're offering 50 percent off the price of tickets and people feel very good about the brand in Australia because of it. Sometimes you just have to think, you just have to make potentially irrational business decisions in order to protect the brand. This story hasn't been told in England, the last day I was there I stood up in front of a whole barrage of cameras and said 'this is a very sad day, we can't get the competition authorities to behave in the way we think we should, we've been made this fantastic offer and we've decided to sell out. I'm afraid it's going to mean 7,000 job losses, it is going to mean the doubling of airfares, it is going to mean you're never going to see a low-cost carrier down here again, but at least I've got a quarter of a billion dollars to take back to England so something positive has come out of it', and I held up the cheque, and then paused and said 'just joking'. There was a deathly hush when I

1

Virgin loves to, we all love to, take industries and shake them up and make sure they're never the same again

said I was going to sell out and then I just said 'look I want you to realize how you felt in the last minute, and I want the competition authorities to realize how the public would feel if we had sold out. We will never sell out; low fares are here to stay and we're going to get out there and compete' and I ripped up the cheque. From our staff point of view, that was a fantastic, positive statement and for our other companies in Australia, like the mobile phones, it was a tremendous boost. All the time you must make sure you don't do anything to damage the brand; every move you make must be one that enhances it rather than the reverse.

The best way of getting people to be enthusiastic about something is to create either the best quality in your field or the best value in your field. In Australia, Virgin Blue is giving the best value, in the UK I believe Virgin Atlantic is giving the best quality. First of all, people must make sure that what they're giving their staff to do is something they can genuinely feel proud of, they can generally feel they're making a difference, otherwise there's just no point in doing it; having done that, communicate well with them. A big recession is just coming up at the moment. As best you can, try not to lay people off, do job sharing or send people on unpaid leave but don't take the easy option of losing people.

Key executives who are quite capable of running their own company within a bigger company, should be incentivized enough to become multimillionaires. If they can create a lot of money for a company, we shouldn't be afraid of them having a stake in it. Virgin has made nearly 100 millionaires or multimillionaires. I think if we hadn't done that Virgin wouldn't be the biggest group of private companies in the UK today. Never begrudge people; never begrudge writing out a cheque for £75m to one person – once that person has made us £500m. We're getting profit share schemes throughout our groups and I think that is important as long as it doesn't become something that people expect as part of their wage packet at the end of every year. This really is a genuine profit scheme so that people realize that if it's a bad year they're not going to get anything but if it's a good year then they're going to get something.

There's no question that Virgin Trains has been the biggest potential challenge, not only to the brand. It was a big risk that we took when we took it over four years ago, but we knew we could turn it from the worst to the best. A year from now we will have done so. The biggest challenge has been carrying the staff with us through the years when we were being knocked by the press and knocked by the public. The trains were getting older and more and more dilapidated and so I spent time writing to them, communicating with them, meeting them, having parties with them and listening to them, making sure they know when the new trains are coming and involving them with the new trains, giving them uniforms they feel comfortable with – that they actually like wearing, rather than impose uniforms on them. I remember going to a back room at Euston where the train drivers and people meet while they're waiting for their trains. It was the most despicable thing; British Rail had given them a horrible place, a hovel of a place. I decided to spend some money on giving them television to watch whilst they wait for the trains, games to play; again, treating people as human beings and encouraging them to keep in touch.

If we hadn't taken the trains on, nobody else was willing to do it and nobody else was going to invest in it. I think that sometimes in life you just have to take risks. I personally believe that if you turn the clock forward five years and you are writing a book about brands and asking 'what was the biggest difference that Virgin made to this country?', people will point to the trains, something which, right now, people would say is the biggest risk we took, the most damage that we've had to the brand. But Virgin loves to, we all love to, take industries and shake them up and make sure they're never the same again. We've done it to the airline industry, we've done it to the financial services industry, we will do it to the rail industry.

Gordon McKenzie

Brand Quality Director

I'm Group Brand Quality Director, which is a title Richard came up with. It's all to do with customer service because that's what Virgin is renowned for. Initially it started off working with Richard trying to sort out trains to get a more consistent level of service. Then Richard asked me to look at Virgin Express in Belgium which is a challenging place to run a business. It's very difficult in terms of dealing with unions and has the highest employment costs in Europe. Then we started Virgin Mobile – we had a tremendous uptake and problems at the call centre, customers not being able to get through and not getting their phone calls returned. Now I get involved in starting up new ventures, to put the right people and processes into place. About 18 months ago I started the customer-service group to spread best practice. I got all of the customer-service people from all of the companies, all of the managers who have customer-facing staff working for them. We sat down and thought 'we've got people here who walk the talk, why don't we use our people for training?' So that's what we do now, every three months we have three or four different subjects – like how to build relationships with the customer – and we have Virgin Atlantic or Virgin Direct come in and say 'this is how we do it'. We found that when we started new companies they would go off and get some consultants in to advise them about the whole Virgin culture, which is great until you discover that the people that they got in have never dealt with Virgin. That's a bit wacky.

As a group we are getting together a lot more. Human resources have a meeting every three months, Will Whitehorn has a marketing directors' meeting, the finance guys get together, so do the IT guys. There is also a channels forum which includes all the companies doing businesses over the web, and then the call centre group, because we've got at least a dozen call centres in this country. We get them into a room and say 'well what are you guys doing and what are you working on. What are the issues you are facing?' A lot of what I do is facilitate so that if somebody says, 'we've got this problem', I say 'well don't go out and hire a consultant I've got somebody at Virgin Atlantic who does that, we will see if we can borrow him for a few days'. So we'll get the customer-relations lady from Virgin Atlantic to do a course for the people at Virgin Express, for example. The goal is to try and treat the customers the same.

Virgin brand extensions

Everything Virgin Atlantic does spreads to us. They spend a lot of time identifying the qualities of their best people and their recruitment is about trying to mirror those best people. We're trying to spread that message across the group. We're looking for happy, bubbly people because you can't put that into people. Obviously training people to work on Virgin Trains is very different from Virgin Atlantic but being happy, being upfront is all part of it. Rewarding and compensating people is another thing. We have a scheme at Virgin which works very well based on five indices: our customers, working well together, attitude, getting things done and Virgin professionalism. That's how they judge all the people in the organization and you're rewarded on that basis.

It gets difficult as you get bigger. As the guy in Virgin Atlantic says, 'our challenge is going from a great little airline to being a great big airline' and that is more difficult. There are obvious things like at Virgin Atlantic they do the 'back to the floor' thing every year, on the anniversary of the company, so that this year, for example, the MD was working in the post room; Richard was working on the customer help desk – unfortunately giving everybody upgrades! We also have what we call an employee scheme called Tribe where everyone is allowed a discount on all the Virgin companies as well as other companies that we deal with – so you're part of the tribe.

Virgin Trains started something called the 'great service awards' to try and focus people on what we're all about and recognizing that some people do it naturally, some people need a little kick in the backside. The first prize is, say, a holiday in America for you and your family with spending money. You also get to have dinner with Richard. The customers select it; you can pick up a leaflet at the stations, and on trains, so if somebody has impressed you, you can nominate them for a great service award.

Chris Green, the CEO joined about two years ago. One of the first things he did was introduce the customer-service council which brought together all the customer-facing people in a room every month to say 'let's look at the complaints, let's see what we're doing wrong, why are customers upset and let's look at changing those things'. That's something that we've used in the last six months at Virgin Express and it's great because people who thought they never had any kind of input and even if they did nobody would pay any attention to them, are now making the decisions. The proof is they haven't had any complaints for months, which is fantastic.

I think it's about picking the right people to run the companies because we've got a lot of really good people that lead from the front. Again, there's not many people in this organization that I can think of who sit in a great big office, it doesn't work like that. We're looking for people who are open, an open style of managing with open doors. If you go to Richard's office, you will notice that he doesn't have a door, which can be a bit awkward at times!

That's the whole thing, empowering the staff, monitoring them – so they know how they are doing – making it easy for the customers to complain, so they tell us what is good or bad, motivating and communicating with our people, satisfying them and the customers and, at the end of the day, hopefully, you get the kind of style that you want. We have 30,000 people, but they're all in little companies. Our philosophy is if it gets too big, break it up so that you get that entrepreneurial culture again. If I have one lesson, it's use your own product – experience what your customers experience. I sit on Virgin trains every week – no one knows it's me – but that's the way I get to see if it's really working.

Will Whitehorn

Corporate Affairs Director

When I joined Virgin, we had this idea of quality and value for money innovation. Also, Richard always wanted to do things with a sense of fun. We began building up in our minds ideas that everything Virgin did should be about innovation, competition, value for money, quality and fun, and we needed to put the personality into the brand, because Richard was going to have to fight battles to get the rights to access he wanted. So when we restructured Virgin we decided we would create five rules for ourselves and wouldn't be embarrassed about putting Richard's personality right to the fore. We now know exactly where we're going with this brand. We really have become a branded venture capital organization. One where we've chosen core areas of investment and we're now going to build those businesses around the world using the brand, using the management experience and using both our own capital and partners' capital, be they venture capitalists themselves, institutions or trading companies that want to be in the business we're in.

Virgin is very good now at starting businesses from scratch with joint venture partners, like the Virgin One account or Virgin Direct, but we were not good to start with. We are now also good at restructuring businesses. One of the things that Virgin Trains has taught us is that the brand challenge is even deeper than we thought. We knew when we took on West Coast Mainline that it was a five-year project; we couldn't produce the vision of the future unless we could get the structure of the company right. But what we underestimated was the sheer difficulty of turning round that juggernaut of a state-owned business and it took us a year longer than we expected. Interestingly our research shows it hasn't damaged the brand at all in the eyes of the general public. It has hurt us with opinion formers but that's a very short-term thing. We believe that by 2004 it will be seen by marketeers and opinion formers as the best thing Virgin ever did and the most natural thing in the world, just as in 1984 going into the airline business was seen by the marketing press as an absolute disaster and Richard was off his head. Now it's seen as a natural extension of the brand.

We had no choice about the Virgin brand name, that was part of the deal with the government, we didn't want to use it until all these new trains arrived. They cleverly insisted, because they knew we would have to work much harder than anybody else as a result of having our brand name there. We were taking on 3,600 people who were used to one way of doing things. We invited them to big parties at Richard's house, 15,000 on a weekend with all their other colleagues from the Virgin companies and their families, and a series of events like that. Richard put a lot of effort into the people side of the business, really getting the staff to understand the philosophy of what we were trying to do with the business. Giving them the kind of exposure to where we were going with the business plan which a normal company would not do. Explaining how the upgrade deal with Railtrack was working, what the economics of the business were, how it was going to go out of subsidy in a certain time, how we had to double passenger numbers and why. Why we were increasing fares here yet cutting fares a lot there. How yield management works, so all the staff began to understand. How the new trains were being ordered, and how customer service had been put into the heart of the way the trains had been contracted with the manufacturers, unlike any of the other train manufacturers who were thinking of buying trains. We rewrote the way we ordered the trains and we explained this to the staff. So they have a really good level of knowledge about what the company is doing and the struggles it faces. And they've been very supportive during an incredibly difficult period where the rail industry has been in crisis. Keeping staff morale high through this crisis is proof of the resilience of the work that was done two and a half years ago.

We now have a Virgin Charter in terms of customer service linking with recruitment, HR and public relations – all working with the brand standards. We have set a series of ideas around which the brand should work and that every action the company takes in every area should buy into these principles. So when Virgin One recruits people for the call centre or Virgin Mobile recruits people for its Trowbridge call centre, they incorporate these principles into the recruitment programme.

The relationship we have with the general public has to be at the core of what we do and that stretches into every area of our organizational structure and the way that we behave with the outside world in every respect. No company could ever live up to 100 percent achievement; the thing is to try and when we fail say sorry. And I think that kind of honesty is the core which we try and incorporate into the companies – that's the way they've got to behave with their customers.

We don't separate customer service like a lot of organizations do. When corporate finance are working on developing a new business and a new model, we are part of that process with them. I read business plans and understand the modelling techniques, how asset finance works. So our people who are in our corporate finance department have to think, 'what's the impact on the brand of this business decision?'

Everything that's facing the customer is holistically managed. For instance, Virgin Atlantic is organized so that the HR director is an advisor to the customer services director, who not only has the cabin crew but also the catering operation and contracting – which we've now done at Virgin Trains as well. So the customer services director is responsible for all the elements that interface with the customer. Therefore you try and create an holistic experience for everyone and that will mean they'll come back for more.

We have set a series of ideas around which the brand should work and that every action the company takes in every area should buy into these principles

The new trains for Virgin Rail, unlike any other train order in the history of railways, was based on airline principles. We didn't order a train, we gave the manufacturers a timetable of services we wanted to run, journey times we wanted to achieve, the reliability levels we wanted to achieve, the noise inside the train that had to be achieved, the smoothness of the ride that had to be achieved, and we said if you come up with a box that does it fine, but these are the things you have to achieve for the customer. And that was what the entire order was based on. The first complete output-based contract in the rail industry! Not only that, but they had to maintain the trains throughout the life of the franchise as well, so whatever products they put into these trains, they had to maintain them and they only got paid on the basis of the maintenance contract as well. The only way they'd make money out of the contract was to take the whole thing. What we did was basically give them a design for the train – just a picture of what we felt it should be like inside and then Priestman Goode worked that up with the manufacturer, and the train we got is identical to the one we drew in every respect.

Richard's one of these people who will take responsibility for the actions of the organization in a way in which a lot of bosses of organizations would not. Because he's lived with this brand since he was 17 or 19 years old, it's like part of his family to him. When he goes on holidays to Necker Island he takes Joan and the kids, but he takes over 120 employees over six weeks every summer. And there's a group of cabin crew of the year who have been nominated by their peers to go. The staff like the person they work for and that makes a huge difference, it makes a huge difference to their perception of how they've got to behave as well.

One of the models that we've looked at, because we've done a lot of work on this issue, is the John Lewis Partnership, which has maintained a fantastic ethos of the way that people work and has remained one of Britain's most successful retailers.

My advice to anyone is don't try and look at an organization like ours and think that what we've done with the brand is the right way to go because it's very unlikely that the same set of unique circumstances will ever come together again with a brand in the near future. But do think about all the things that we've done and try and put them into the context that you're in. There are things that we've done that in your own context could be really quite successful. Don't make promises you can't keep. Try and incorporate the idea that what you're doing is looking at the individual customer and build a business round them.

2

PizzaExpress started in 1965 because founder Peter Boizot was 'fed up that he couldn't get a decent pizza in London'. His vision 'to serve the world with style' still drives the company today so that each of the 286 PizzaExpress restaurants in the UK and 29 international outlets is unique in style whilst offering a 'reassuringly predictable' experience across the brand.

The flat hierarchy, strong performance management and absolute attention to detail have enabled this award-winning organization to grow revenues and profits in the last year by 24 percent whilst continuing to retain loyal customers, 22,000 of whom belong to the PizzaExpress Club.

The directors are passionate about 'walking the talk' with customers and employees and spend at least three days each week in-store. The company values and operating philosophy are instilled in new managers through rigorous induction training programmes and regular attachments to stores.

PizzaExpress was the first and is still the market leader in its sector. This has been achieved by a culture that has successfully managed to sustain the individuality of the brand whilst continuing to achieve a highly consistent customer experience. The organization, which currently employs 6,000 staff, seems to be on track to achieving its long-term target of 500 outlets in the UK and Ireland.

Ian Eldridge

Chief Executive

I've spent 13 years working alongside Peter Boizot and most of the things I notice in restaurants and say to staff are probably as a result of his style and vision which is 'To serve the world with style'. In 1993, when we became public, we amended that vision slightly 'To serve the world with style, at a profit'.

This vision determines how we run the company. We are control freaks. I'm obsessed about customer service. Customers, quite rightly I believe, expect us to have at least the same standards they demand on the high street. I welcome that because I think catering in the UK is generally poor. What we try to ensure within PizzaExpress, right across our estate of restaurants in the UK, is that there is a reassuring and predictable nature to each visit. Yes, we screw up on occasions, but I think as long as our communication lines are open and people like myself and our chairman, David Page, get to hear about it we can put it right; we don't hide behind some customer services director. I am the customer services director. For example, our PizzaExpress Club has over 22,000 members who write to me, email me and phone me, on a very regular basis with their experiences. Some executives may see this as a pain but I don't. I have some 22,000 additional 'area managers' out there who tell me when the ladies' toilet doesn't flush properly! Customers are really surprised when you write back or phone them over the weekend to tell them what you have done about it – they can't believe it.

The members of the board all consider themselves to be experts in everyone else's field. Our PLC meetings would make a wonderful fly on the wall documentary! We're fascinated by the detail. We discuss price reviews, menu content reviews; it's pretty wild. But most of my time is spent with customers and staff out in the restaurants. I turn up unannounced wherever possible. I don't like to think that staff have had a chance to move the rubbish from the fire exits! I want to see it 'warts and all' because that's what the customer sees.

Our vision 'To serve the world with style' starts with design of the restaurant – every one of our restaurants is different. We don't subscribe to the cookie-cutter approach where you take 4,000 sq foot and drop in the current PizzaExpress layout. For a start, it wouldn't be fun. David Page, as chairman, plays a very active role in design within PizzaExpress. We try to be the restaurant chain that's not a chain and to make sure every restaurant is different.

Once the restaurant is designed, we generally don't rework it over its life span, apart from maintenance. How it was designed is how it stays, unless there's a very good reason to change the style. You find that customers all have their favourite PizzaExpresses and they often ask me which my favourite is. I say it depends on what the weather is like, what day it is, who I'm dining with, whether it's lunch or dinner and what mood I'm in. I have many, many jewels in the crown.

'Uncommon Practice' at PizzaExpress

14-week induction and orientation programme for new managers

CEO personally corresponds with PizzaExpress Club members

Chairman plays active role in design

Each PLC director has five adoptive restaurants

Waiting staff keep their own tips

Good promotion opportunities

Local charity schemes

Local education schemes

No PAs or offices for directors

We have a very high frequency of repeat business particularly by our PizzaExpress Club members. We encourage them to revisit with various vouchers and with birthday promotions. If we're opening a new restaurant, they are encouraged to go and visit the new restaurant and report back with their views. They tend to write every week to say which PizzaExpress they have visited or which Café Pasta they've been to during the previous week.

Given that the restaurants themselves can vary enormously in terms of their style, we try to make the product 'reassuringly predictable' for customers. Take the menu for a start. You don't see many of our regular customers reading the menu; they generally know what they're going to order and that is great because if they are creatures of habit and if they feel comfortable within that environment, then that's terrific. But then the customer will be specific about how they would like their egg cooked in the Pizza fiorentina or whatever! And I think that's right. If I hear a waiter or waitress in PizzaExpress say, 'That's what the food manual says it should look like or how it should be cooked', I say 'Yes that's the standard, but you're dealing with customers and they have expectations of how their experience should be. We have to at least match those expectations, but I want you to exceed them every time'.

The employees also have a big role in creating the reassuringly predictable experience. It doesn't matter what I say or what David Page says if a customer goes to PizzaExpress in Uxbridge today and the management is not on the floor or the staff are not presented well or ready for business, then it impacts on that experience. The customers may forgive us because they've previously had 25 years of PizzaExpress experience and it's always been a good one. But if they visit Uxbridge and have a poor experience, and they go again a few weeks later and it is no better, then they are going to deduce that PizzaExpress in Uxbridge is slipping. Then they conclude that PizzaExpress as a group is slipping.

We have an incentive scheme whereby waiters or waitresses keep their own tips. You generally don't see adverts for waiters at PizzaExpress, it's a hard job, but our staff love it. We are not only in the customer-retention business, we are in the staff-retention business.

We're heavy on induction. There are loads of manuals and pictures as to what the product should look like. There are videos too, which feature Peter Boizot talking about our ethos. It's like an extended family. If you've got 1,000 staff joining you every year, which is typically what we have with 30–35 restaurants opening every year, it's difficult to get that culture across very quickly. Managers receive 14 weeks of training. It's very tempting to chuck them in at the deep end. Sometimes deep-end training is good but once they're in that particular mode it's very difficult to pull them back for proper training.

We don't have a marketing director because marketeers dream up ideas about how you can spend money. We enjoy spending money, but in a controlled fashion to generate profit, which is basically more people sitting in our restaurants. We like to think that every experience customers

2

We like to think that every experience customers have with PizzaExpress is promoting and advertising the product

have with PizzaExpress is promoting and advertising the product. Word of mouth is by far and away our biggest marketing medium. Clearly one way of driving new business is to get the public to try PizzaExpress through Sainsbury's with our supermarket offerings or by drawing them into our restaurants at off-peak times. That is one of the reasons why Peter first started the live music evenings and our jazz club. He saw it as a way of bringing in 50 people on a night that normally would be quiet. There are maybe 30 restaurants that present live music now, although not necessarily jazz.

We also help communities, be it the National Trust or a local cause. For example, a special pizza may have been created and for each one sold we will donate 25p to a local church or whatever. We play a very active role with schools. In the early years our promotions person would invite a school into the restaurant, so the children could make a mess with the flour and dough and all sorts of stuff but now we delegate it down through the system and you find the restaurant managers are performing that role. Not only is it fun but they realize it's a way of bringing new customers to their restaurant, because the children make the pizzas themselves, show mum and dad, the school teachers are generally impressed and there will be pictures in the papers.

In terms of keeping our brand alive and sustaining the customer experience, the other key is consistency. Customers will say the pizzas are different in St Albans, well they are because they are handcrafted and made by individuals. In Welwyn Garden City you'll get a different pizza at lunchtime than you would at night time. But there are certain fixed parameters within which we operate; this is the reassuringly predictable offering that we have. Most of the competitors out there can be good; I've had fantastic experiences but I've had some pretty lousy ones too. The challenge is consistency, that's why I admire Pret A Manger. You very rarely find a queue there, they are very quick and their eye contact is fantastic! The theatrical experience of Pret is remarkably consistent. That's why if I'm peckish at three o'clock in the afternoon in town I go to Pret.

I can measure the business by speaking with the restaurant managers. I worry if a restaurant manager does not know how much business they did last night or if he doesn't know his customers or which their favourite table is or who their favourite member of staff is or how they like their pizza cooked. We generate management accounts every four weeks in arrears so when I find area or restaurant managers saying 'oh well I don't know how we did because I'm waiting on management accounts'. I say, 'you should know how you did – the management accounts are a confirmation or otherwise of what you should already know'.

PizzaExpress is a very simple concept. Sometimes people try to make it complex and it's not. In the early days in the UK we had franchises and they would be concerned with the level of business. I'd ask 'what sort of comments do you get back from the restaurant?' and they would say 'oh I don't go to the restaurant, I just read the weekly reports'. Each PLC director has five adoptive restaurants so that we can break through any structural barriers and the washer-up knows he or she can talk freely with a director. It sometimes annoys restaurant managers when you ask the washer-up what's not working. As a PLC director we'll just get it fixed because the guy can't operate without hot water!

My ambition for the brand is that in every capital city around the world there will be a PizzaExpress, Café Pasta or San Marzino, which is increasingly becoming our international brand because PizzaExpress in certain territories conjures up a perception of home delivery. The standards of the past 35 years, and especially over the last eight years, have been moving steadily upwards. We're constantly challenging ourselves. Call it arrogance, but within PizzaExpress we genuinely believe we can turn our hand to any aspect of hospitality management.

James Parsons
Managing Director of Restaurants

We promise to consistently offer all our customers a good pizza, served by pleasant, amiable, well-trained staff in clean, well-presented restaurants. We keep it simple. The brand isn't just the pizza or the people. Sounds obvious, but the style and presentation and the ambience of our restaurants are important parts of the brand too. You will find visiting PizzaExpress many things that are on brand – it's about clean lines in the restaurants, tables, chairs, plants and pictures on the walls. We complement that with a simple menu. It's a menu that we've been running without serious overhaul for many years. Keeping it simple helps to keep it consistent.

We also have a relatively low turnover of managers and staff, so we are not training new people in the business over and over again; rather we nurture our existing staff. The majority of our managers used to be a waiter or a chef or a cleaner in the business, so they know exactly what it is that we hope to do for our customers. I don't know if this sounds a bit corny but we try to treat our staff like people. We don't talk about it, we just get on with it. A lot of companies say that they have mission statements and all sorts of values for how they deal with their people but I sometimes wonder if they're not spending a lot of their time talking about how they should look after their staff, rather than just getting on with it and being a decent, honest, open employer. Our chairman is an often-used example as an employee who started out his PizzaExpress career as a washer-up. Not everyone wants to go on and be the chairman or area manager, but for those that do there are great opportunities.

The people who are coming into our organization all receive a superb induction, orientation and training in the company. I joined about three years ago. I had been in the catering service industry for 16 to 17 years, so I had a fairly good level of experience and knowledge but I still had to go through a three-month programme. I spent four weeks in the kitchen making pizzas each day, working as a cleaner, working on the restaurant floor, working beside experienced people in PizzaExpress and for some time running the restaurant as well. This happens at all levels of management, whether it's me coming in as a relatively senior manager or it's someone coming in

2

You just have to be clear what it is you're setting out to do. Don't make it too difficult and complicated, then make bloody sure you do it!

as a 20-year-old assistant manager. The induction and the first few weeks are extremely important. The people on the restaurant floor are key. When you think back to good visits that you've had to a restaurant and you ask yourself why that visit sticks in your mind, it's usually because of the service. You tend to forget how good a steak was or how good a pizza was or how clean the toilets were – those things sometimes become secondary to service which is the main issue.

I spend two to three days a week in the restaurants, so I'll have a couple of days of office work then the rest of my week is in the restaurants with the people, both front and back of house, the managers, the waiting staff, talking to them to get an idea of what's going on, what's good, what's not so good, getting the general tempo of what's happening in the restaurants.

We have just stuck to what Peter Boizot started doing in 1965. It's a menu where there's a sensible choice on the starter and pizza section and we don't do burgers or steaks. We hope to do pizza well, that's what we set out to do. We feel that if we start doing burgers and everything else, all we will do is dilute what PizzaExpress is about, which is serving a decent pizza over and over again. Other people try to cater to all possible parts of the potential customer base, we don't.

It's fine to do it consistently well over a dozen restaurants, but then you have to do it over some 280 restaurants. That is a challenge we have in the UK. The next challenge we have, as we progress internationally, is to ensure that what we do in the Strand is repeated on the Champs-Elysées or wherever else around the world. But we are helped enormously by going back to the values I was talking about before, in terms of keeping it simple and clear.

What I have learned is that you can't please all of the customers all of the time. So just try and please most of the customers all of the time. An example is PizzaExpress doesn't do children's menus as you would know them, like McDonald's or Pizza Hut do. We are a bit more of an adult environment. We could do it but at what cost? We might put off customers by putting too many children in the place and then we'd be competing against people who do it extremely well already. You just have to be clear what it is you're setting out to do. Don't make it too difficult and complicated, then make bloody sure you do it!

BANYAN TREE

HOTELS
AND RESORTS

3

Banyan Tree is a luxury chain of 10 hotels, 13 spas and two golf courses, which has been consistently voted not only Asia's best resort hotel but also one of the world's most innovative hotel chains. Its compelling brand benefits, romance and intimacy are delivered in lush, tropical environments, through staff renowned for their very personalized level of service. There is a sense of theatre and drama at Banyan Tree – the experience is summarized by its strapline 'sanctuary for the senses'.

The chain employs over 2,500 people who are encouraged to stay in the villas to get a real sense of the memorable experience the customer will enjoy. Estimates of US$30 million gross operating profit and revenue of US$55 million in 2001 clearly demonstrate that Banyan Tree's strong brand proposition, well marketed and consistently delivered, is a recipe not only for countless awards but also for financial success.

3

Ho Kwon Ping

Chairman

It started because we were primarily resort developers but when it was time for us to build the final resort, in Laguna Phuket, we decided to get into hotel management ourselves. We wanted to fill a gap that we felt was missing in the marketplace, which was a kind of 'smallish' hotel experience that would be very romantic, that would not be luxurious in the normal definition of 'luxury'. Instead, it would be very strongly reflective of its location and surroundings, and one that would leave you with an extremely memorable experience.

Once we decided that we were going to run our own resorts, we discussed our ideas of what that resort experience should be. Certain values came through as imperatives for us – romance and intimacy, for instance, and how that could be reflected in the design of the resort. One of the things we joke about but in fact take very seriously, is our pool villas. The Banyan Tree pool villas are one of the few in which one can safely walk around naked – and nobody would see you! You are in a world of your own. That was one of the challenges we set ourselves when we created the Banyan Tree – to create a world that envelops and cocoons you as a guest.

This challenge involved impressing a strong sense of immediacy and location. Once you enter a Banyan Tree resort, your past is suddenly put away and you are in this special world. We brainstormed and discussed the types of experiences that a guest could enjoy from morning through to night. The Banyan Tree experience was shaped more from what we thought a customer might want than any particular service standard we would adopt, such as the standard telephone etiquette of picking up the phone within three rings.

Since no such resort existed at the time, we couldn't do a lot of market research. Instead, it became a very personal thing for those of us who happened to be of the 'baby boomer' generation. We extrapolated from our own travels and holiday experiences, and we took it from there. Building a hotel from scratch was a slow, painstaking process, but working with a blank canvas was a great advantage for us. It allowed us to break the rules.

In the Banyan Tree Spa, for example, we abandoned the whole idea of air-conditioning and our original spa consultants thought that we were crazy to even consider it in Asia. Instead, we put our spas in pavilions within the lush tropical settings, for which the Banyan Tree is now renowned. What were the key steps involved in creating a great customer experience? For us, the physical design is very important – we have evolved so much in terms of what the latest Banyan Tree villa should be. In our newest resort in the Seychelles, for instance, every villa has a pool. We're just introducing a spa and pool villa concept in Phuket which includes a special pavilion within your villa compound in which you can have your spa massage and lots of other spa experiences.

'Uncommon Practice' at Banyan Tree

Staff encouraged to be creative within a given standard

In-house interior design and architecture facility

Staff encouraged to address guests by first names

Staff stay the night in a villa to sense the experience

Pre-opening parties for everyone involved in a new resort

Exchange programme for service staff

Two brand managers: one in marketing; one in operations

Intimate Moments Package

Sandbank Affairs programme

In this villa, the bedroom is set amidst a lotus pond and is fully enclosed by glass. It has electrically controlled curtains, so that you can close it off if you want to. But the bed is not even a bed. It is basically a beautiful platform in the middle of the room, a perfect square. Traditional hoteliers would say that beds must be accompanied by strong reading lights as found in every major hotel. In the Banyan Tree, we have created other spaces for guests to read within the villa. To us, the bed should be more like an altar. The bed is made like the Thai 'dang'. In the day, beautiful cushions and a wooden server adorn the platform, so that you can relax and eat or drink there. At night, we turn it into a very romantic bed overlooking the lotus pond. Very oriental in concept...

When we first started, we were quite differentiated but the marketplace today is far more crowded and there are many smaller hotels offering something similar. However, I think the fact that we have the in-house capability to create the entire experience gives us a decided advantage. A big chunk of that capability comes from having our own interior design and architectural people who have been with us for a long time and who are a strong part of the team. We do an enormous amount of brainstorming and when we do a new project or create a new product, we spend a lot of time on all the little details that go into creating that guest experience. I believe that by doing it this way, it is far more considered and we can try to anticipate every part of that experience from the beginning to the end.

A good example of this is our Intimate Moments Package. It's a package for couples, which one member would usually order as a surprise for the other. He or she would call us before they go out for dinner and, whilst they are away, we come into the villa and transform it into something totally magical and quite theatrical. We place satin sheets on the bed, light up to 50 candles all over the room and open a bottle of wine. We run the hot water for the outdoor bath, light candles and lay out a whole tray of aromatic massage oils for you to choose from, towels and so on. You then return to this incredibly romantic surprise and do what you're supposed to do...

In a way, if you take the theatre analogy, the set design lays the stage for each guest's own piece of interactive theatre. We can't write the script for you; you, as guests, are going to create your own stories. We structure the setting, shaping in some way how you are going to behave. Having created the setting, our staff are then trained in all the basic elements of any five-star service establishment – how to greet guests, how to remember their first names, how to anticipate their needs. But we also try to get our staff to understand that their role is to get the guest to actually act out their romantic fantasy. We have a programme of getting all our staff to stay the night in our villas so that they get a sense of what it's like – otherwise it's very difficult for them to know how they can help our guests create the special experience they want.

This, in a way, epitomizes what the Banyan Tree is about. It's not just about a beautiful setting, it's not about luxury that is opulent or grand. It's all about creating an environment and an atmosphere that is quite special, and then acting as facilitators for each guest's own out-of-the-ordinary

3

That drama,
excitement
and sense of
participation
is what I think
drives us all

experience. It's the kind of thing you would probably giggle at if you were to do it yourself but it's lovely to have someone set up a bit of theatre for you – and to me a good hotel is a bit of theatre.

Our service style is very much infused with a sense of Asian grace, with a strong emphasis on the natural environment. It's a very sensorial experience, encompassing scent and even sound. It's never clinical. For example, our Thai spa therapists would continue to keep their hands on you as they move around you very lightly on bare feet. That would drive some spa consultants crazy. Many believe that spa therapists should have white uniforms and white shoes, but a big part of Asian grace is the soft sound of bare feet. We also burn incense of your choice. We transform a massage into a complete Banyan Tree experience.

The Banyan Tree promise has impacted on how we work as a team. We try to involve as many people as possible in the creative process – brainstorming, designing, redesigning and talking through what we want for a particular project or new product, and the kind of standards we want to set. We work hard as a team conceptualizing and implementing our ideas. This is best captured in our pre-opening parties; the celebratory parties the day before a new hotel opens. Everybody who has been involved comes together. The sense of participation is so strong and the excitement so palpable, it always reminds me of the final dress rehearsal before a play. We sometimes worry that everything hasn't quite come together before opening night, and we're not sure if it all will. When opening night finally arrives, magically everything just comes together! The audience is out there and the curtains are pulled back! That drama, excitement and sense of participation is what I think drives us all. It feeds that sense of drama and theatre that defines the Banyan Tree – we create settings. We help our guests become the players who can act out their stories.

The Banyan Tree experience or proposition, if you like, may not affect the way we recruit people, but it certainly affects the way we evaluate them. The people who work at the Banyan Tree, particularly those involved in planning and management, are not only disciplined and proficient, but must also able to participate in pretty earnest dialogue and to push their point of view. In other words, I believe that you have to be really passionate about your beliefs and ideas.

Outside of passion, pride is another key component of being part of the Banyan Tree team. Pride in making a big difference – in knowing that a particular job would not be done if a particular individual were not around. It's a sense of personal responsibility as well as being a good team player.

Now that we're getting bigger with 10 properties, we have just started an exchange programme for our service staff. We have also introduced brand managers: one on the marketing side and one on the operations side. Now that the organization is getting bigger with more people, the challenge is to have people who really understand the brand, with a good sense of how to put it into operation. We find that standards do vary in the different locations but the challenge for us is to maintain some of the differences that make each resort distinctive and evocative of its location while maintaining that overall Banyan Tree experience of theatre, romance and intimacy.

Bernold Schroeder

General Manager, Banyan Tree, Maldives

When it comes to administration in our resorts, we have very strict rules but at an operational level, we allow flexibility for creativity and sensitivity. For instance, the room boy understands that when he turns down the bed every night, he has to leave the standard hotel gift behind, but he is given the freedom to decorate the bed with a flower, painting or anything else he believes would create a fitting greeting. In this way, we are still able to amaze someone who is a frequent visitor to our resort!

Over the last few years, our brand proposition has really impacted on the way we develop our service staff. We're not necessarily looking for people with previous hospitality experience but more specifically, people who are creative and with a natural friendliness and desire to make others happy. A good example would be Hussain, a Maldivian who started with us as a junior waiter. Most hotel operators would not dream of putting someone with his experience in charge of a major resort programme like our 'Sandbank Affairs'. But he has used his creativity and flair to create an incredible personalized dining experience for guests.

Hussain sets up a beautifully laid table surrounded by torches and candles on the ocean sandbank; he writes little notes and poems on the sand to welcome the guests. He arranges for a fisherman to catch a fish for the couple's dinner, for the boat crew to play traditional 'bodu beru' music whilst the guests are dining, and even has snorkels on standby in the event that couple decides to swim before or during dinner. What's more, he'll walk into the water with a bottle of champagne to quench their thirst if necessary. At a minimum price of US$400 per couple, he carries a major responsibility in ensuring that each experience is unique and memorable.

He is able to do this because he isn't just a good waiter but a smart all-rounder, able to create a bit of theatrical magic for our guests.

Abid Butt

General Manager, Banyan Tree, Phuket

Our resort operations are synonymous with a theatre production. The management team are the producers and technicians; our guests are the main protagonists, and our service staff play a supporting role in helping them realize their stories through the delivery of a very personalized level of service. This is evident, for instance, in our Thai wedding ceremonies which are conducted in the romantic setting of the couple's villa. Our staff play an integral role on these special occasions, not only in guiding the ceremony but also in the decoration of the villa, arranging the post-ceremony meals and spa treatments.

Oxfam

4

Oxfam is a development, relief and campaigning organization dedicated to finding lasting solutions to poverty and suffering around the world. It looks at the symptoms and campaigns on the underlying causes of poverty, working with poor communities, partners and supporters to help every human being to have a certain amount of decency and dignity in their lives, equipping them with the skills necessary to support themselves.

A confederation of different organizations around the world, in the UK alone there are 23,000 volunteers, 1,300 UK based staff, 1,500 overseas staff and 600,000 donors – their combined effort raised over £120 million in the year to April 2000.

People at Oxfam are emotionally involved in their work and care is taken to make sure that individuals at all levels of the organization have a voice. The brand, and the values attached to it, influence and affect the way people at Oxfam work – its authority, its involvement of others, the way it's working to empower people and the fact that it's ingenious are the four brand attributes that distinguish Oxfam from any other organization in its field.

4

John Sayer

Executive Director, Oxfam International

The belief behind Oxfam is that all people on this planet have the right to a certain amount of decency in their lives. What might distinguish Oxfam from some of the other charities working on poverty is that we look at the symptoms as well as the causes, however complicated these may be.

We have a collective mission statement, two and a half pages long, that has focused our message. Then we have a paragraph-long positioning statement, which is for our own communications. It's particularly difficult for us, when compared to a coherent single organization, because we are a confederation of different organizations, with different histories, which started at different times, and which exist in different societies, and have to communicate with these societies in their own context. Considering that, I think we've done quite a good job of having a fairly coherent message with a common brand.

We are moving to the consciousness, the understanding that we speak with one voice and, whatever anyone says, it will have an influence on all the rest. We're all more aware of how the brand takes on, and absorbs, value like a sponge.

It astonishes me just how successful commercial companies can be in building the loyalty of their employees to a product. With an organization like Oxfam, people are emotionally motivated by what they see and what they read about people suffering around the world. Many of the staff and volunteers working for Oxfam think they're in an incredibly privileged position to actually be able to do something. They feel incredibly motivated to want to help people who are really disadvantaged, people who are in deep trouble, children who are ill and have diseases which can be cured. They can help and actually be paid for it. Other people have other jobs but give money to Oxfam and in a way I am as impressed by the people who donate money as I am by the staff who work hard for Oxfam. Staff don't feel a sense of powerlessness at how much is wrong with the world, they feel you can actually do something. It can be quite uplifting.

What distinguishes Oxfam specifically? We're quite careful about making sure people have a voice at all levels of the organization. People care deeply about their work and they need to be heard, so it's not a top-down organization. There is quite a good balance of listening throughout, with a lot of consultation, but not to the point where we are completely paralysed by processes and committees and meetings. People feel we challenge ourselves constantly, we don't have a fixed approach to helping people. We're constantly seeking to renew ourselves, we invite challenge from our partners in developing countries and we ask 'are we doing the right thing?' We invite challenge from the public; we're happy to debate with government on what's the best way forward for overseas development. We are not part of an establishment that will just carry on and not ask the difficult questions. We must challenge ourselves and everyone else who claims to be responsible for reducing poverty. And I think that creates a certain loyalty and a culture of being open minded and participatory.

'Uncommon Practice' at Oxfam

People have a voice at all levels of the organization

Flat, non-hierarchical structure

Administrative staff get the opportunity to visit projects in the UK and overseas after a number of years

Annual Oxfam Assembly weekend for representatives

In a business world we would be like business units, except without a boss at the top. I'm not the boss. I am a peer to the other executive directors. But it helps being a confederation because we're fully able and willing to challenge one another. There are slightly more conservative elements, then there are the slightly more radical elements. For example, should we be inside the halls of the United Nations and the multilateral meetings negotiating our specific policies or should we be out on the streets with the protestors and the ordinary people shouting about injustice and haranguing the world leaders who are turning up for these meetings? I don't think it's written down in our values, it's just part of the way we've always worked. There's a tremendous lack of cynicism in Oxfam, we really care and we really worry. Are we doing things right, are we helping, are we making a difference, is the world becoming a fairer place, are we contributing to reducing poverty? If it's getting worse, would it be even worse if we weren't doing what we're doing, how can we do it better?

Our people are critical to Oxfam. Firstly those people looking at the policy issues and doing advocacy, lobbying the rich and the powerful, and suggesting new policies and ideas. Then there are the programme staff who are working directly with people who are in a state of poverty or insecurity or injustice. The crucial challenge, to an organization like ours, is to make the link between the two and be clear that this must be a two-way, backwards and forwards linkage. For example, the policy changes that we are advocating at high level in the United Nations with national governments must be based on issues and problems that we've identified at village levels.

The third group of people in the organization are the marketing people. Increasingly we need to raise money and funds, but that is also a process of raising people's awareness and understanding. We want to appeal to people's intelligence and their minds as well as to their hearts. We don't want them to see miserable looking children with skin diseases with their hands held out. We work against the image that they are helpless and that if you give money to them they can succeed. We are increasingly saying they have every capacity to help themselves given the right opportunities.

Finally, there are the administrative staff. The trick is to make sure that the administrative staff do the kind of tasks that would be done in any commercial or public organization. In Oxfam most people get the chance after a number of years to go to a village and visit people. To me, there are two things that are highly motivating in Oxfam. One is to go to a village and meet ordinary people, the women, the children and the men. The mere fact that you are there means things are changing, things are getting better, you're working with them, they've got plans, they're doing more irrigation, they've built a clinic, they've built a hospital. Life is getting better and so out come the musical instruments and everyone has a dance. That is tremendous – it really recharges your batteries from the days you spend in the office simply working on the word processor. The second thing that is equally motivating in my experience is to go and give a talk to a school or to young people. Young people are idealistic and you see a really good side of people in this line of work. I worked in Hong Kong, which has a reputation for being a place where people are interested in one thing, and one thing alone, which is making money and getting rich. I gave talks in schools and it

4

was great to see their enthusiasm for helping other people, to see that Hong Kong people were willing to give money to help in Somalia, Sudan and Ethiopia, places they know almost nothing about. We raised millions and millions of dollars. Talking with schoolchildren about poverty issues is just as motivating as going to the villages and seeing the villagers celebrate that their lives are getting better.

We need to put all forms of economic organization, whether they be social, democratic, capitalist or socialist, at the service of making people's lives better, and that's really our starting point. We must get better at talking to and interacting with companies. There are companies out there who realize increasingly that they have a social responsibility but are not quite clear what that means and what they should do about it. They are increasingly approaching us and saying 'what can we do?' and I believe in many, many cases this is not window dressing, this is not public relations, this is an honest approach to say, 'well, where does our future lie in terms of our social responsibility?' And they have vast resources. If we can turn that goodwill into positive action for change, for a more equitable world, where more people have rights, it becomes mutually advantageous. Everyone will be better off, including the companies. Companies don't like poverty any more than we do in terms of their own success. They have very little to gain through poverty in the long run. We have to learn to put capitalism in the context of human development.

Having the brand has helped us strengthen our message. It's all about communication and being able to communicate using old and new technologies. You need an identifiable presence; you need to try and stand out, to attract people's attention. In the old days it might have been standing in Oxford town hall in a tweed jacket, giving an intense speech in a very academic way, and people would say 'my goodness, these Oxfam people know what they're talking about!' Today we know it's about having an identifiable logo that appears on websites all around the world, on advertising hoardings, on TV. It's still all about communication but having this single brand globally. We know the media are global, so that an image published in one country can go all over the world, TVs sell it, the web is borderless of course, newspapers are increasingly globally produced and so are magazines. We want people to know about us because we think what we do is good. The brand is relatively young, we've only had it a few years, but I think many of us within Oxfam understand that the brand is the quality of our work, the quality of what we do. And if what we do is good and people understand that, they will remember it and link it to Oxfam. If we don't have a clear, strong and simple brand, they might see what we do but they'll forget who it was that did it. They see us supplying water during some terrible war situation in eastern Europe or Africa, they see us doing projects within our own communities with various deprived areas in the north of England, they see us talking at the United Nations asking for actions not words, and all the time they see that logo and they will just remember to aggregate those things and say 'yes that's what Oxfam does'.

It's rather like the dream catcher that native Americans use. Capture those things in your brand. I don't know your definition of branding but I always start with a logo. I know branding is much more than that but I start there and then realize it means your identity, your public image, how people perceive you. We need a simple message, we need a simple front door, through which people can understand the more complex aspects of what Oxfam does, which is what we do with poor people in villages and slums in hundreds of countries around the world every day.

John Whitaker

Director of Marketing

The brand is an instrument in fixing poverty. Oxfam's programme is made up of three broad elements. We do rapid-reaction work on emergencies, which probably has the highest profile. We'll try and build long-term solutions into this work, but very often it's about life saving and it's sudden and urgent, and although you can plan to respond, it's very much a rapid-reaction set of activities. The majority of our programme work is in development programmes to build sustainable long-term solutions where people can work their own way out of poverty. That takes years, but it's working at the grass roots, establishing good community based communications on programmes, that enable people to find solutions to their own poverty. The third area is in advocacy, where the obstacles to people getting out of poverty are all in infrastructures. Whether they are local, national or international, it's the rules and regulations, the policies and the practices of governments and international institutions or of corporations, which provide the barriers.

One of the best examples of that is within trade, but it's probably the most complex. It's very apparent that trade barriers, whether they're inside a country or internationally, have an enormous effect on the lives of villages in all sorts of places, whether they know it or not. From the experience we have on the ground, campaigning and lobbying for change to global regulations is a major part of the programme. And campaigning is where the brand really comes in. It doesn't really matter if you're working in a village somewhere in Africa or Asia whether they are aware of the brand. There, it's about a personal relationship. It doesn't matter too much if you're in a refugee camp which brand of clean water you're getting. If you're getting clean water and your family doesn't have cholera – that's all you're interested in. But when it comes to building a global movement you need to be able to cut through the communications. It's at that end of the work that the prominence of a brand and the values that are attached to it are vitally important. What you want to say is – 'This is Oxfam, a leader in anti-poverty work, and it's characterized by its authority, its involvement of others, the way it's working to empower people and the fact that it's ingenious'. Those are the four brand attributes that, in combination, distinguish us from other organizations in our field.

The fact that we invented a special form of bucket doesn't sound terribly inspiring, but the bucket is a really good example of ingenuity. It saves pots of money in emergency responses because it's designed to be transferred cost-efficiently. In West Africa we didn't invent the fact that you can farm water by building little walls along the contours where rainfall is scarce – it's caught behind the walls and you can plant things and get a better crop. But years ago we did invent the way of local people being able to do it themselves without calling a surveyor in at huge costs – this was just having a plastic tube and two sticks which were marked with a height measure. Put some water in the tube and you can use it as a level and work out where the contour is, build your wall along the tube and move on.

In advocacy as well, it's about finding clever ways of bringing things to people's attention. We were campaigning on IMF policies a couple of years ago and started producing adverts and little packets of medicines, which were labelled 'IMF, bad medicine for poor people'. It really got up the nose of the IMF to the point where they started talking to us, because they were so angry with us, and it was the first time they ever really engaged with non-government organizations.

The brand and our beliefs influence and affect the way we work. We were offered £1 million by an oil company which was pitching for drilling rights at the time and we turned it down flat. It's easy to walk away from £1 million. Just try not to dream about it afterwards! Support, however, is very much wider than funding. For example, we believe that a company like BP has policies and practices which are extremely damaging to both people and the environment around the world. But we work with them to try and improve their behaviour and we believe that there is a serious commitment within that organization to do better. But we would be reluctant to take money from them, because that would compromise our position.

We will choose over and over again to work with organizations in ways which can be particularly empowering. In Vietnam, where the whole coast is affected by cyclones, there is a very flat sea plain, which gets flooded every year. Over history the Vietnamese people built sea dykes to protect themselves from the cyclones. The Americans bombed them during the war as a means of destroying the North Vietnamese economy and they were never reconstructed because nobody ever had the resource to reconstruct them, so 25 years on there was still desperate hunger and starvation in North Vietnam. We worked with a programme to rebuild the sea dykes – we could've gone in and just built sea dykes or paid people to go build them – but what we did was work with the local communities. There are no charities or non-government organizations, it's a party structure and government structure parallel in Vietnam. But working with the lowest levels we could of government structure, the village and local communities, people were paid enough to live on for a year whilst they rebuilt their own sea dyke, in ways that they could maintain and sustain them afterwards. We arranged support from Hanoi University, where necessary, to relearn the skills that their parents and grandparents had of building dykes and harvesting mangroves sustainably, because they're the outer defences that live outside the sea dykes. That sort of approach, the way in which a programme is developed, is driven by Oxfam's values.

While our brand is a vehicle to achieve our beliefs, it's also all about people. It's the people that we're working with and the people who work with us – whether they're employees or volunteers or as partners. It's a very people-intensive organization. The concept that drives our fundraising is

The concept that drives our fundraising is that 'we work with others to help them help themselves'

that 'we work with others to help them help themselves'. That's all about our people, their people. The distinguishing feature for us is 'working with', and that is about saying that they need accompaniment. Long-term solutions to poverty won't come out of aid alone, they won't come out of strictly giving to people. Long-term solutions come out of people finding their own mechanisms to survive and respond to their environments. Take the Vietnamese dykes. We don't go in and build them, we don't even manage the process. It's the community that manages the process, but our programme officers will be accompanying their organizations, offering them advice, and drawing from a global experience too.

When I'm asked about the passion within the people at Oxfam, the domestic examples in the UK are good. We have some 20,000 shop volunteers, on whom Oxfam is hugely dependent. We have about 20,000 activist campaigning supporters who are convinced that they can make a difference to global poverty. And we have about 600,000 donors who are giving their money. And in each of those populations there's a hierarchy of involvement. Some people are more forward in giving us their opinions than others, more involved, more active – those people need to be involved. When we're making changes we go through what sometimes seem to be interminable consultation processes. Every single time that has happened the proposed solutions from the management have been materially improved by being wide open to people who may disagree deeply with what we're saying. As a manager, you can't possibly find solutions that will meet everybody's needs. But listening genuinely improves results.

Recently we sent 20 of our staff, each clutching a certificate for one share, to the Glaxo SmithKline annual meeting to ask awkward questions about their pricing policies in poor countries. The reaction of any board at their AGM to being asked probing questions from the floor – they only ever do it once a year – seems to be a mixture of terror, open resentment and anger. But Glaxo SmithKline are responding in changing their pricing policies and thinking more about their public and their customers than they would have been had they not been campaigned against.

In Oxfam, we have such meetings with our own people all the time. I was up in north Wales last week at a meeting of volunteers in a church hall in Colwyn Bay. We're looking at rejigging the way we get donated goods round our shops. In our 800 shops around this country, 600 of them get enough across their doorsteps to sell; 200 of them don't. They're in pedestrian precincts or somewhere where it's difficult for people to drop stuff off. So you've got to move the stuff around. We think we're spending too much money on it. We think there are different ways of doing it and that's going to involve some changes and the changes will probably mean that some depots could close, some people could lose their jobs. This hasn't been announced yet but the rumour mill is working pretty well. I had a church hall full of shop volunteers, who were deeply concerned about the issues and really concerned about the people they work with and what their future is, and whether people are going to lose their jobs. I was being challenged, and rightly, and I was learning from it and I'm sure that the things that were being said there will help us. Being accountable and being open is what I'm talking about – it's not something where we're happy with our performance, but I think we are ahead of much of the commercial world.

Legally, we are governed by 12 trustees who are volunteers; behind them is an association. We have created an assembly of about 200 people who are representative of all our different constituencies: our shop volunteers, our staff, our donors, our activists, supporters, the programme people, the beneficiaries and so on. And we get together once a year and we're accountable to that body. All the key elements of the organization, the people who are managing it have to account for themselves and explain why they're doing what they're doing. And they get challenged pretty hard sometimes.

Gill Holmes

Campaign Volunteer, Oxfam GB

I've always been a volunteer, I've never done any paid work for Oxfam. It would be about eight or nine years ago I started volunteering. We just do everything really. I'm a teacher by profession and finished working in November to spend more time with my young children. I wanted to spend a bit more time as well doing stuff for Oxfam, so at the beginning of this year I helped the Manchester office with the publicity for a conference that they were organizing on asylum seekers and since then I've set up a group in Stockport to support asylum seekers. I lobby my MP regularly; I do campaigning, fundraising, letter-writing, lobbying and I've also set up a fair trade group.

Most people in Oxfam can get really incensed about the rights and wrongs in the world and can get quite angry. You'll find they're very passionate about how unfair the world is and they want to do something to right those wrongs. We feel angry that the world is such a wrong place and our government is influential and we can influence it, therefore we should.

Generally speaking for lobbying, and certainly for lobbying new MPs, the information you get from Oxfam is very specific and very detailed. The contact briefings are superb and very precise, very prescriptive if you like, but with enough background information so that you can make it your own. And that I think they've perfected really well. If you're campaigning or running a stall, there are always postcards to sign or some petition to sign or postcards to send to the Prime Minister or whatever. So that the materials the general public sees are the same and the posters that the public sees are identical. This creates consistency from campaign to campaign.

The Oxfam Assembly is the best example of the organization communicating. It's basically a gathering of representatives from every aspect of Oxfam's work. We meet for the weekend and work very hard getting to know each other but working as well and learning an awful lot. Absolutely everybody is there, the director, all of the trustees. I went and I just sat next to somebody for a meal and had a good chat with them and then afterwards realized how immensely high-powered some of those people are. People who are doing amazing things internationally, people from Oxfam International or from other Oxfam sister organizations, people who are working in the most dangerous war zones or whatever it is. And everybody felt so equal; it really was your ideal example of what equal opportunity should look like. There were men and women, young, old, black, white, it really didn't matter, and whatever position people actually had in life was totally irrelevant. We were all there with a shared purpose. And I felt very strongly that everybody's contribution was welcomed and was valued and felt equal. We were inspired by each other rather than by any one particular individual; there wasn't any one person who was greater than another.

Owen Bieth

Campaign Volunteer, Oxfam GB

I first became involved with Oxfam on an active basis about 30-odd years ago at university. After that I was involved in various other things until about 11 or 12 years ago when I wanted to get involved in campaigning activities. Oxfam has become a much more focused organization, the level of information and research I found to be particularly impressive; there's no question that the information is there to back up Oxfam campaigns but at the same time I feel that it has become a little bit detached from some of its more grass-root activities.

We find that we're very much campaigning in the abstract as local people. But when we've been collecting signatures for landmines' petitions we've had people come up to us and talk about their own experiences in their own countries. People from Israel and Cambodia actually came up to us and told us about their own experiences with landmines. Most recently, during the Gujarat earthquake emergency appeal we were shaking cans at the stations and somebody from Somalia came up and said that he wanted to find out more information about how he could make a donation on a regular basis to Oxfam because when he fled from Somalia he had been in a refugee camp where Oxfam had been working to provide the clean water supply; I think that's one of the most satisfying moments. Obviously you're campaigning on the issues but it is very gratifying, very satisfying to feel that little bit of impact, that little bit of feedback that shows that what you're doing is having some impact somewhere, you're contributing towards helping make other people's lives just that little bit better than otherwise they might have been.

MIDWEST EXPRESS AIRLINES

The best care in the air.®

5

Midwest Express is a small airline with a big heart. Its slogan 'The Best care in the air' is demonstrated every day on the business routes it serves in the USA. It is one of the very few airlines that has been consistently profitable over the past 14 years during a period when the airline industry has lost billions of dollars.

Midwest Express innovated premium class seating and freshly baked cookies on board its commuter aircraft. But more than anything else it is the people of Midwest Express that have created the brand. The management pay enormous attention to creating and sustaining a culture of care in the air by caring for employees. The airline has grown but that growth is carefully controlled to ensure the culture of the organization is protected.

The airline's success is evidenced by the numerous awards that it has collected over a number of years including being voted Best US Airline for six years in a row by Condé Nast Traveler magazine. No mean achievement for an organization of just over 3,000 people.

5

Tim Hoeksema

Chief Executive Officer

We coined a phrase many years ago: 'the best care in the air'. It's a lot more than just a marketing slogan. It's something that we know we have to accomplish and have to live every day if we want to continue to be successful. We're a tiny airline, operating in an industry of giants. The only competitive weapon that we have is customer service. Taking that phrase 'the best care in the air' and achieving it is really the key to our success.

When we were designing the airline more than 17 years ago we offered two-by-two seating, all of them first class seats. Because nobody likes a middle seat we got rid of them and gave more leg-room. We offer a great meal service. We bake chocolate chip cookies fresh on board. All those things are part of the product offering, but it's much more than that. You can choose the restaurant that has the best food but, if you don't feel welcome there, it is not a good experience. I'm asked many times, 'What's the secret to your success?' Well we have over 3,000 secrets to our success, and they are the terrific people who make up our team. Our people have to understand that accomplishing the 'best care in the air' goal is critically important to our continued success. They have to understand how they relate to that, and how they affect that.

We are differentiated by our seating and our food but much more so by the way our people take care of our customers and respond to them. We try to be honest and direct if there's a flight problem or a delay, and to communicate frequently and regularly. We are a niche player focused on the business traveller. There are many decisions that flow from that decision. The schedules we have, the time of day we leave, the room to work on board the airplane, complimentary newspapers in the morning, complimentary coffee in the gate area and our service all focus on our target market. When deregulation happened in '78, and on through the early 80s, the business was awful. You couldn't pick up a newspaper without reading about deteriorating service, pulling service out of small communities and airline mergers. In our opinion, the needs of the business traveller were not being met so we set out to fill that void in the marketplace. Our service offering to our customers is totally consistent with who our target market is, with our strategy as a business and with the niche that we choose to fill in the marketplace. We've been consistently profitable for the last 14 years. There is only one other airline in the USA that can say that and that is Southwest. From '90 to '94 the US airline industry lost in excess of $13 billion. Only Southwest and Midwest were profitable during that period.

We developed a set of core values that are every bit as important today as they were 17 years ago. The first one is service to the customer. We want to treat each customer as though he or she were a guest in our own home. Second is respect: respect for the customer, for employees and for vendors. We want to treat everybody with respect. Third is responsiveness. We're in a very

'Uncommon Practice' at Midwest Express

Open, listening environment

Orientation and diversity training for all recruits

Two-day workshop to reignite the spirit of service culture

Awareness Weeks programme

Quarterly 'Talks with Tim'

'Chameleon' training

First class seats for all passengers

Chocolate chip cookies baked on board

---

competitive industry; we have to be very responsive both externally in response to outside pressures, and internally in dealing with each other. Fourth is honesty and integrity in all of our dealings with customers, with employees, with vendors, with everybody. Honesty and integrity is an absolute. We have worked very hard at applying those values.

In the hiring process we look for people who have the same core values that we have as a company. We devise interview techniques so that we hire people who have our values. You have to model your values. By role-modelling our values, by setting those standards, we're saying, 'This is the way we operate here'. We create an environment that's open. People can speak their minds. I think that leads to honesty and integrity. People have to say what they feel, and they have to feel safe to do that. Creating an environment in which employees can say whatever comes to mind can create ideas.

The chocolate chip cookie has become virtually a trademark for Midwest Express. People say, 'You're the company that bakes the chocolate chip cookies on board'. It's funny; the chocolate chip cookie was really a part of a cost-saving effort that we initiated when we were a year and a half old. When we first started, we served a great big meal on every flight. Our afternoon flight left Milwaukee around 3:30, we served a big meal at around 4:30, and landed at 6:00. We decided we really did not need to serve huge meals at 4:30 in the afternoon, but we were afraid to stop.

One of our employees said, 'I've been thinking about this, why don't we serve chocolate chip cookies and bake them on board'. I said, 'Oh, that sounds like a wonderful idea!' I have to tell you that baking at very high elevations is very different. Instead of baking three dozen cookies at a time, our flight attendants bake eight or nine or ten dozen cookies in a tiny little oven at 6,000 or 7,000 feet cabin elevations. It took us about six weeks to perfect this. We never had a single complaint, and the cookies became a trademark. We saved $85,000 a year because we listened to one of our employees.

We really do try to create an environment where we can listen. I listen to the people who report directly to me, but I also listen to the people who report indirectly to me and encourage all of them to listen to each other. The really good ideas generally don't come from me. They come from people at the point of contact, where they're talking to the customers all the time, and they just observe and say, 'Here's an idea'. We don't do a lot of measurement, but we do measure. The groups design their own measurement systems and measure themselves. How long it takes to get a cup of coffee on a flight. They say what you measure is what you get.

When we hire people we start them in orientation. Everybody, no matter who you are, has a couple of days of orientation and a day of diversity training. At orientation we talk about our company. We talk about our brand and our history, and we talk about what has made us successful. We talk about experiences and give examples and share stories. If you really want to perpetuate the culture of an organization, the important thing to do is to tell stories about it and to give living examples of what's important to the organization. So we communicate constantly, share stories, share examples and share thousands and thousands of letters.

We have a learning and development department that provides 'chameleon' training, as we call it, for handling different types of customer situations focused on providing the best care in the air. You can do all kinds of training but the stage is probably better set by example, by leadership, by the management and supervision of the company. Employees see decisions made in favour of the customer and us scrambling to be sure a flight gets out on time, and they learn very quickly that, 'Whoa, this is a company that means what they say! So I'd better hustle, better get that bag off…' Just maintaining that culture is something you have to work very hard at.

As you grow and get bigger and get more and more people, if you aren't careful to control your growth rate, you can have a little drop in terms of your performance. About a year ago, I felt that we were starting to see a trend down, so we did a large group interaction to focus on reigniting the spirit of our service culture. We had 300 people in for a two-day meeting. They were a cross-section of the entire company. We listened to our customers, too. We brought in a group of 18 very frequent fliers. You could have heard a pin drop while these customers were talking. We had a cross-section of a group of employees and we listened intently to them and you could hear a pin drop there, too. We asked, 'What is it that we have to do to support our employees better?' From there it cascaded through the whole organization. We heightened awareness and refocused on the importance of delivering good service. I really feel, based on the data, that we have gotten our focus back.

If you want to be promoted here, it's important to be known as someone who really focuses on customer service. There are just two kinds of employees, those who deal directly with the customer, and those who support those who deal directly with the customer. We're trying to help our people in the finance area understand that what they do has a very important effect on the customer. If the employee is having trouble getting a payroll check on time, or refunds are slow, that impacts on how that employee takes care of the customer, or they have an effect on what day the customer gets their refund. Over the years we've been successful with Awareness Weeks. We've had Flight Attendant Awareness Week, Maintenance Awareness Week, Finance Awareness Week and Station Awareness Week. That's when anybody in the company can sign up to go work a four-hour shift on the ramp as a flight attendant, go to the hangar and shadow a maintenance person, or work in finance. It really enhances the appreciation for, and the awareness of, what other people are going through.

I have quarterly 'Talks with Tim'. I go over to the hangar and I have three different meetings, one during the morning, one late in the evening, and one midday, so we cover all of our technical service systems. It's just an hour and a half open session of Q and A, and I just get some terrific questions, and enhance people's understanding. It helps me to stay plugged into what's going on.

I do that in January and in February I do it at the airport with customer service, and pilots, and flight attendants. In March I do it at the headquarters. In April I might do it in Kansas City, or I'll be back at the hangar. I circulate around every quarter to our main places of employment and do these open chats that are very effective at keeping communication open. It helps, because you have direct customer contact people and indirect customer contact people all together in these meetings so you can understand another person's position.

There's not a lot we would have done differently over the last 17 years. You always have to be very careful that growth doesn't get away from you. We've had about a 14 percent compound annual growth rate in the last 10 years. A few years ago some airlines were growing 150 percent a year. With our product, and our focus on the customer and service, we could never do that. Our constraint to growth has not been capital. We've had all the capital that we would need to continue growing. It's really been our perception and our ability to maintain the customer focus, to maintain the quality of our product. Customers constantly tell us, 'I wish you went here, I wish you went here'. Growth is important, but you have to balance that aspect of customer service against all of your customer service.

My advice to other senior executives is to be sure you are meeting customers' needs. See if you can differentiate from what's out there in your product or service offering. Be sure that there is a common vision that is felt by all of your employees. As you bring people on board, choose people whose values are consistent with the values you have. Be sure that they're accomplished; look for the best people you can. Then be sure they all have a common vision. If you get the best people you can, they are all heading in the same direction and they are all focused on the same important things, you've gone a long way towards accomplishing what you want to accomplish.

Chris Stone

Senior Vice-President, Human Resources

The role people play has everything to do with delivering the brand so we write it into our 'employer brand' positioning statement. 'In the same way that the external brand promise of Midwest Express is about providing the best care in the air, our employer brand is built on a foundation of caring. We care about Midwest Express, the little airline born of our past, coming of age under our watch, and shepherded into maturity by future generations of employees. We believe that service is the secret to our success and that a caring work environment for our employees is expressed in the service we deliver to our customers'.

As we develop operational excellence in a customer-intimate model, what matters more than anything? From our people's standpoint, what do we have to do especially well? Do you have to do performance management pretty well? Yes, you have to do it, but it doesn't have to be 'state of

God forbid the people of Midwest Express would wind up behaving like everyone else in the airline industry!

the art'. What about pay and benefits? No, you don't have to do that incredibly well. You do have to meet people's needs and you do have to have some flexibility, and those sorts of things. But more than anything, what you have to do really well in a customer-intimate environment is to hire the right people. You must then develop well and then give people the support and the tools and the freedom to make bold service decisions. That's what we're learning to do. I would rate our hiring as second to none. It takes a long time to get hired at Midwest Express, but it takes a long time to get hired at most really great customer-intimate companies because they need to be fussy about whom they hire. To become a flight attendant here you almost have to be Mary, Mother of God. The flight attendants really care that they do not let anyone into their ranks who can't deliver. It's a passion and that's true in other areas of the business as well.

We orient people carefully. I don't think there's any other airline – in part because it would be impossible, but also in part because they don't value it – that would fly a relatively low-paid ramp employee from a remote city airport to Milwaukee for two days of orientation. We do because it matters so much. There's a double loop in that learning. When people arrive and undertake that orientation, they know that they've been treated differently from any other role that they've ever undertaken in life. They're rather shocked about it. We continue to shock them, since we have their attention with the first jolt. There aren't very many businesses in which the CEO comes to orientation and meets with new people. Our orientation process is not about benefits. It is included because you have to cover it somewhere, but a lot of it is about our culture and the things that make us different. Most of this stuff has evolved from the core DNA. God forbid the people of Midwest Express would wind up behaving like everyone else in the airline industry!

Tom Vick

Senior Vice-President, Marketing

I always say that airplanes are cold, metal machines, and it's the people who deliver the warmth and service. The market research we've done shows an enormous differential between the next competitor and our airline in terms of customers' ongoing preference and what they repeatedly buy. It goes back to the consistent delivery of the product so that the business traveller knows what to expect. What we provide is a premium product in a commodity business.

The people you interact with affect the customer experience. The individuals who are delivering service are the key differentiators because, basically, the aircraft are the same. So, it's the training that those individuals receive. It's their understanding of what the brand is all about, the brand promise, what they need to deliver, understanding what part of 'best care in the air' applies to their role, and knowing that when you're on stage, you're on stage, and you perform. We go through a lot of role playing so that individuals can actually see the journey a customer goes through with regard to 'the best care in the air'. Obviously, you have a variety of individuals in these new orientation classes, anything from a person who works on the ramp to a pilot. It allows them to be exposed to the full culture of who we are, and what's also impressive is that at the end of those sessions, all of the strategic leaders within the company are there to greet that new class. I've seen sessions where four people are in the class and 30 senior leaders are there welcoming the individuals to the company, talking about how important it is that you're here, that you've made it through our recruiting, and that we hired the right people to implement 'the best care in the air'.

Cliff Van Leuven

Vice-President, Customer Service

The 'oomph' is
what we have to
go out and find

I spent 20 years working for a major airline that didn't have a brand so it's fascinating for me to work at Midwest Express, a company that has a clear and laser-like focus on the brand promise of customer service. Everywhere an employee looks, they're reminded of what we're about. I can't think of a theme or a brand for the major airlines that's going to lock customers into those carriers. The frequent-flyer programmes are a hook, but they're a meat hook. It's as though they're saying, 'You'll fly with us because you're going to go on vacation and this is going to save your family a fortune when you stay in the hotels that are affiliated with our frequent-flyer programme'.

The difference is in having employees who know what the brand is and what the promise is. When things are going badly we provide customer service. Not too long ago we had turbulence on a flight, and the flight attendant spilled red wine on a businessman's shirt. The flight was coming out of the east coast, so the cockpit crew called Milwaukee and said, 'We need a shirt. We think the guy's about this size'. Somebody from Milwaukee station went to Kohl's, the local department store, and picked up three shirts. When the plane landed, we were standing there with those shirts for the customer. We agonize about our training. The things that we need from our people are not learned in the classroom. You've got to have the right energy. I call it 'oomph'. Those are hard things to teach. We can refine their skills, but we're not the kind of organization that can just bring someone in to punch keys and pass out boarding passes. They must be able to say, 'Good morning! How are you today? I see that you're going to Los Angeles. Do you have any luggage to check? We have coffee and newspapers for you down at the gate. Is there anything else I can do for you today? And thank you for flying Midwest Express!' So we have to hire that and refine it through training, and then we'll teach them the technical skills. The 'oomph' is what we have to go out and find.

Our customers tell us, it's not the airplane, it's the CEO and the people that he hand-picks. Then it's the people who those people hand-pick for their positions, and then the flight attendants and customer-service folks that we hand-pick to deal with our customers. So here we are with our little DC-9s competing with the likes of Northwest and their huge network and aircraft here in Milwaukee, and we carry more customers. It's our people.

6

Harley-Davidson is one of the most recognized brands in the world today. Its products are so distinct that the company even investigated registering the sound of its engines but decided against it because there was no need – there is no other bike that sounds remotely like a Harley-Davidson.

Its customers are famously loyal with over 45 percent of owners previously owning a Harley. In fact, they say the only reason a bike enthusiast deserts the Harley brand is through death or bankruptcy! What other group of customers willingly have the product logo tattooed on their body?

Harley-Davidson does not sell motorcycles – its brand vision is 'we fulfil dreams'. Over 600,000 customers worldwide belong to HOG (Harley Owners Group) and spend their vacations and weekends riding with up to 25,000 other riders at a time. A significant part of annual revenue comes from merchandise, clothing and events.

The senior executives of the company ride their personal bikes with customers, sharing barbecues, stories and beers. They call it 'Super-engagement'! Harley-Davidson is 100 percent customer experience.

John Russell

Vice-President and Managing Director, Harley-Davidson Europe

I think the thing about the Harley brand, like all great brands, is we started out with a great product that, in our case, was a motorcycle. The founders of the company didn't sit there with a brand plan in that shed in Wisconsin in 1903; they decided they wanted to design a motorcycle. That motorcycle took on certain characteristics which then determined the product experience: how the motorcycle feels, how it looks, what it sounds like. So all of those things begin to evolve into a product-related experience for the customer. Most companies don't go much past that. The experience that most companies talk about is actually an extension of the product attributes and strengths or, maybe in some cases, its weaknesses. I think the thing that Harley has always been able to do is to create this sense of engagement with the customer through the basic attitudes of freedom, individualism, enjoyment, self-expression, self-confidence; a whole range of words you can use to describe this rugged individualist, this independent thinker, this person that chooses his or her own course in life. Most people have a defining decade for Harley-Davidson, it might be 'Easy Rider' or something more recent, but there's always a sense that the underlying qualities of freedom, individual experience, individual behaviour, self-confidence, however you describe it, are wrapped up in a contemporary characteristic that adds to the satisfaction of the brand experience.

We got into brand extension at a product level through motor clothes and accessories and licensed products, not because they were an opportunity to stick our name on something else and sell it to the customer, but primarily because they were an opportunity for the customer to broaden their connection with us. They wanted to do these things; they wanted to be able to signal their connection with us, their engagement with us. Having the events side of what we do creates opportunities for customers to demonstrate what they feel about the brand and do things that make them feel connected with the brand. They've all been born of this very organic process of feedback that we've had from customers.

We actively engage with our customers; we encourage our people to spend time with our customers, riding with our customers, being with our customers whenever the opportunity arises. We have a very positive engagement process that gets our customers wanting to talk to us. The culture within the company is very much the empowerment model that many other people would subscribe to, but I think we probably do it more effectively than I've seen it done in any other business. This means that within the company it's very difficult for a good customer-driven idea to get lost in the management mechanism. If it is important to the customer, if it's a good insight, if it's a good point of understanding and connection to the customer – it does actually make its way through into the business process and become part of what we do. Our value system is all about the individual, it's about openness, it's all about encouraging contribution. Our business process, the way in which we structure the company, the way in which we make our decisions is always drawn from this

'Uncommon Practice' at Harley-Davidson

Open, non-status culture

Stakeholder philosophy

Harley Owners Group

Harley world tours

The Open Road Tour

Induction programme for recruits

concept of understanding what's out there, whether it's the customer issue, whether it's the dealer issue or employee issue. We have this balanced stakeholder philosophy that says as we go through our process of developing the business, we do it for the shared mutual benefit of all of those stakeholders. And it's not a piece of plastic; it's not words stuck on the wall. So nobody would make a decision without first evaluating the full implications of that decision and that means thinking about all of the stakeholders in the process.

What this requires of me is spending a lot of time with the organization itself, ensuring that the system we know works so well is perpetuated, continued. It's all about individual leadership. It's all about me spending time with all of my stakeholder groups in terms of ensuring that things in Europe are done in a way that is cohesive with world strategy but also meets the needs of the stakeholders within the European business: our customers, our dealers, our employers. It actually makes operating the business quite easy because you're dealing in the world of certainty and information. The more you engage with customers, the clearer things become and the easier it is to determine what you should be doing.

I think we stand apart from anybody else in terms of differentiation. There are other motorcycle brands that have a cache, have a premium positioning, have a strong emotional element to what they offer and the way they operate, but I think ours goes one step beyond that and it manifests itself in the things we do with the Harley Owners Group. We organize an event and 10,000 people show up. We were at a rally at the weekend in Austria organized by the local chapter and they had 20,000 people attend. The Harley Owners Group now numbers over 600,000 worldwide. In Europe it's just up to 60,000, so a significant number of people. What we have is a large number of people who will actually plan their life activity around what we're doing. People want to know where our events are so they can plan their annual holidays. We've got our 100th anniversary coming up in 2003 and literally millions of people are interested in participating in our year-long celebration, The Open Road Tour, one way or another, whether it's buying anniversary products or going to an event, or wanting to know where the big birthday party will be.

If you move from being a commodity product to an emotional product, through to the real attachment and engagement that comes from creating a product experience, the degree of differences might appear to be quite small but the results are going to be much greater. When you move to an experience where people feel they own it, it's part of their life, it's more like a religion than a product, it's something that's so ingrained in their life that it occupies the same space as the other things that people really value. It's moved from just being a discretionary product purchase to something that is part of the way they are and that connection is so invaluable, so solid. Every company probably has their real brand enthusiasts, their loyalists, but I think what Harley has been able to achieve is that we've made it a very significant proportion of the ownership. We get very few people who move away from our products for reasons other than major lifestyle changes, like they die, or they just can't afford it any more. People very rarely abandon the brand because they've decided to go and buy another bike instead. Our customers are very actively engaged with the brand and almost half of our owners have taken part in one of our major rallies or riding events. Now that's an incredible number if you compare it with the normal marketing measures of programme effectiveness like how many people read your company magazine or how many people fill in a market research survey.

When the company was in trouble in the 1980s, the process we used was not the one that most companies do when they're in trouble – cutting back on the stuff that's really important to people around the business, whether it's employees or dealers or shareholders or customers. Harley took the view that we needed to make the product better, but the big thought was 'how do we get our customers to willingly spend more money with us?' And that is a great thought – it's not a thought that many businesses have. Not 'how do we save money' or 'how do we gain market share or whatever' but 'how do we create more value for our customers so that they willingly buy more of our products and services?' And that was how the Harley Owners Group came into being. The owners' group has never been a marketing cost, it's always been an investment in the relationship with our customers. The conventional process would be a company loyalty scheme and that would become part of the marketing budget and then when the bad times come the marketing budget gets slashed and the owners' experience goes out of the window. With us we try to grow that activity because it's an important source of customer loyalty and that is what ultimately drives our business success. We invest in our customers and we get our return from the various products and services they then choose to buy from us.

We talk about the brand in a number of ways. At a product level we talk about look, sound and feel and those are the attributes that are derived from the product. The products are designed to have this wonderful, sculptured, almost art-like look, the sound of the product is a very distinctive engine sound, a lot of people develop that and tune it to make it sound even more distinctive, the sound of a Harley is one of the great sounds that people associate with. We went through a process of looking at trademarking the sound but in the end we decided it was very difficult and it actually wasn't necessary. We didn't need to register it because it was already ours.

Keeping our brand fresh is fundamental. We keep developing the products. We've just launched our first liquid-cooled bike called the 'V-Rod'. It's actually an amazing bike, astonishing performance, a new look to Harley that is unmistakably Harley but unlike anything else we've seen from Harley before, so it's a very important product for us. At the end of the day, whatever the experience, we have a product that really excites people and makes them feel good about owning it. Beyond that it's all about exploring the potential for developing the experience. The things that are seen as leading edge and totally innovative become the bread and butter of our brand experience. We're developing riding experiences through rentals in holiday locations, Harley world tours, where we take you on an organized tour of self-discovery. Our job is to keep adding to these experiences. What drives us to do that is our customers. We talk about the concept of 'going to the edge of the

We talk about the concept of 'going to the edge of the brand experience'

brand experience' to promote it, so you hold on to your existing customers through giving them an experience that reinforces all things that are good about the brand. We constantly look at the edge of the brand, so there's this constant innovation going on, but it's not revolutionary to the extent that it breaks away from what we do today.

Internally there is this strong focus on the individual working in a collaborative way across the organization. The way we develop the business is quite complex, we're not trying to oversimplify what people have to do, but the direction is very, very clear. In terms of defining the people who work for us, they have to be very strong on empathy. We are a non-status driven organization, there is no hierarchy, we don't have organization charts posted up on the walls, we don't drive the business through a focus on the most important person in the room, the decision gets driven by the business process. Our recruitment process requires us to hire people who can contribute in that environment, and secondly we induct them through a process that's all about understanding the philosophy of the company and the philosophy of the brand experience and the way in which we extend that into all of our decisions. That's the first thing they learn and it's reinforced on a regular basis.

We use the hard measures of how we're doing, because none of this means anything if it doesn't work at the bottom line, so what level are we operating at, what success are we achieving against the competition? We use a lot of the softer measures around the brand; what does the brand experience mean, how is it being interpreted by the customers? We place a big importance on Harley Owners Group measures so, for instance, we measure growth, ie, an event that was attended by 9,000 this year had 1,500 people show up four years ago.

I think you have to be willing to actually abandon things to truly turn the business on its head and say 'we are going to be driven by our customers'. I think if a company copies what Harley does – the physical manifestation of the product – they won't achieve what we've achieved, because behind it is this real commitment to customers, this real sense that the customer is part of who we are.

6

Roy Pinto

Marketing Director, Harley-Davidson Europe

The Harley-Davidson brand is 100 percent experience. There's no rational reason for buying a Harley-Davidson so the experience becomes 100 percent. The bike, the clothes, the accessories, the rallies and everything else that we operate is in support of that ownership experience.

When you're riding a Harley you enjoy yourself, there's always something interesting, there's always something going on, there are always people around you stopping you and talking to you about Harley. You can't park a Harley-Davidson in the street without someone coming up to talk about it. It's difficult to put your finger on exactly what it is but there's something different about owning a Harley or being part of the ownership experience.

Ensuring consistency of the Harley experience across our dealer network is a very difficult job. We have a number of dealer meetings, we have certain operating standards, communication guidelines and we have rules for this that and the other, but we're not a typical car company whereby the dealer has to have a certain type of tile on the floor and every dealership must be exactly the same colour. It's got to look, feel and sound like a Harley dealership to the customers, but none of them looks the same, they're more individualized.

Customer loyalty is very important to us. It's a cliché, but the fact is there is more value to the business caring for an existing customer than trying to find new customers all the time even though both are important. You can write brilliant articles about Harley-Davidson products in magazines and create awareness but when you're sitting in the pub and talking about bikes and swapping stories and hearing about experiences from satisfied Harley customers that's the most powerful marketing there is.

★ PRET A MANGER® ★

7

Pret A Manger is one of the most admired brands in the UK today. It manages to blend passion for food, its people and customers in a way that is both credible and highly profitable. The company was founded by Julian Metcalfe and Sinclair Beecham, two City workers who conceived the idea for Pret when they despaired at being able to find a wholesome sandwich at lunchtime. Since then they have opened 116 stores across the UK and are expanding internationally. McDonald's recently acquired a 33 percent stake but has promised to stay 'hands off' to preserve the unique culture that is Pret.

The company is obsessive about the quality of its food and the ingredients that it uses and places a far higher premium on this than on cost control. It goes to extreme lengths to ensure the quality and freshness of its products. It is this fierce independence that has enabled the brand to create strong awareness in the marketplace and a loyal following of customers despite eschewing most forms of advertising and promotion.

7

Andrew Rolfe

Chairman and Chief Executive

Pret has got a very simple proposition. If you look at our mission statement it says everything you need to know about the Pret brand, that our products are handmade, they are natural, we don't use any chemicals, additives or preservatives and that they are fresh. We make our sandwiches on site every day and every shop has its own kitchen. If the sandwiches don't sell we either give them to charity or throw them away and start again the next morning. So the Pret brand is about great-tasting, fresh, handmade, natural products served by people who are passionate about what they do.

Although our proposition has been clear from day one, I wouldn't describe Pret as a brand. We talk about what Pret is, and about the three things we focus on: that we are passionate about the food we sell, the people who work for us and, finally, our business. The minute you try and separate the brand from the business it becomes artificial. We're not concerned about having consistency of brand so much as about consistency of purpose that flows throughout the whole of the organization. It doesn't actually matter what we write on the napkins or say through advertising, all that matters is that when you go into a Pret shop you get that set of experiences that describes Pret. The way that you interact with our team members in our shop, the way our suppliers interact with us, the way we develop new products and services. That's Pret. Just being very, very passionate about the things we care about.

You can walk into a Pret shop and within two minutes see if the team is working well together, you can feel a positive vibe. It's very clear if the general manager has his team working together, everyone knows their responsibilities, and I'd like to think that culture and sense of purpose flows throughout the whole of Pret from the shop up to the senior management team. Our senior management team have very clear areas of responsibility all focused on a common goal. So if a problem fell out of the sky and landed on the table, without a word being spoken, the right person would lean forward to take it. It's having a clear purpose, clear areas of responsibility and then making sure you have the right people with the right talents that are able to fulfil those areas of responsibility.

Being private we can make decisions that are right for the business, so in November of last year we introduced across the board a wage increase for all our team members, which was unbudgeted, unplanned for; we just felt it was the right thing to do because the cost of living was rising so quickly in London. Funnily enough we increased wages, sales went up and we made more profit. So life does have a certain irony to it.

This compulsive desire of ours to keep making the product better and better helps keep us focused, so somebody will say to us 'Why don't you use guacamole? Why do you use fresh avocado?' In every instance we simply say because it just tastes better when you make a sandwich using freshly sliced avocado and, for us, that is the ultimate test.

'Uncommon Practice' at Pret A Manger

Employee feedback on customer comment cards

Team briefs every morning

Mystery shopper store checks

Shooting Stars voucher scheme

Incentive reward schemes

Pret experience days for recruits

10-day training for all recruits

Graduation pin and pay rise on completion of training

Appraisal and promotion programme

Pret Star magazine

Pub hire for staff on Friday nights

Christmas and summer parties

Tiffany silver stars for customer mentions

Buddy shops for head office staff

Head office staff work in shops five times a year

The second part of our mission is about our people. We've got some amazing people who work for us. There are a couple of things that allow us to have these people. One is the way we recruit. Only 5 percent of people that apply for jobs at Pret get accepted. Candidates have an interview, they then get sent to their closest shop to have an interview with the general manager, after which they are brought back to work in the shop for a 'Pret experience day'. After that the shop team vote and if the team doesn't vote for you, you don't get the job. So already we're creating this team atmosphere.

Business people often find it difficult to understand how we can ask junior team members to make hiring decisions. My answer is that we trust them with our customers every day, we trust them with our business, we trust them with £2.5m turnover every week, so why wouldn't we trust them with hiring their colleagues? These are the best possible people to decide who else they should work with, because they know. You work a bench with someone at 6.30 in the morning, you know who's working and who's not. If managers are quick to criticize the quality of people they employ in their business, they have only themselves to blame. Take our 18-year-olds, what do they know about work? They will work in the way you allow them to work. They have no prior experience when they come to us. They come with an open mind and lots of enthusiasm. So we trust our customers and we trust our team members.

We pay better than the industry standard, so we're able to attract people. But that's not important, what is important is the way we treat and develop these people once they're here. People ask me how do you train your people in customer service? Well, the answer is that we don't. We've got these 18 to 24-year-olds from France, Italy, Spain, some from Africa, and they are wonderful, young, vibrant, colourful people. We teach them how to use the cash register, and we teach them how to make sandwiches and coffee, but the only guidelines we give them about service are greet the customer when they arrive, look them in the eye when you put the money in their hand and make sure you say something when they leave; but more than anything else, be yourself. For example, we encourage them to give free coffee. Sometimes I will go into the shops and the first thing I will ask the managers is 'Are you giving away free coffees?' We say to the team if you recognize a customer, or have kept a customer waiting, do what you think is right.

Every team member receives a bonus every week if the shop hits its mystery shopper target. We have something called 'Shooting Stars': as you are developed in the business, when you pass your various stages of graduation, you get shooting stars, which are cash vouchers you can give to colleagues who have helped you progress. Every Friday night we take over a pub in London which is an open invitation to all of our team members. We typically have over 2,500 people at our Christmas and summer parties. If a team member gets mentioned by name by a customer, one of the management team will visit and give that team member a specially printed Tiffany silver star to acknowledge the fact that they've done something special for the customer. But none of those things matter if you don't deal with people in a direct and respectful way. They are young, talented very energetic people, and we've got to be grateful that they've come to us.

All of this has a direct impact on how we run the business. Let's say I walk back into my office and there are three messages on my desk, to phone an angry shareholder, an angry customer or a team member who's called me from one of the shops. Who would I call first? Like everyone else in the business, I'll call the team member first. That's the most important thing at the end of the day, because I can't really look after our customers. The only people that are good at looking after customers are the team members. The shareholders can look after themselves, so they'll be fine.

Five times a year we clear head office and send people out to work in shops. Lots of companies do that but we don't just do that. We make sure that everyone in our head office has what we call, a 'buddy shop'. My buddy shop is Cannon Street, and I always work there. I know the people and they'll call me on a Thursday night and tell me what the sales performance is. Mary, my secretary, comes in and says my buddy shop needs a new coffee machine, so I fix it for them. By keeping very close to shops, and that means the way we dress, the way we behave, going to the pub on Friday nights, getting involved in the buddy shop, we make the people of the shops realize they're important and that we care and we aren't sitting in some ivory tower making strategic decisions. I don't think we can separate dealing with our people and running the business, I'd like to think they're indistinguishable. And once in a while we'll go and see the bank manager.

Anybody who joins our business at any level of the organization, is sent to work in one of our shops for two weeks. So before they turn up here to man the general ledger even, an accountant has done two weeks in the shop and then they get assigned a buddy store. You'll be amazed how much we learn. Some new recruits think 'oh I've done the head office interviews, this is just a bit of experience', then afterwards we talk to the general manager and the team members who don't know if the person is going to be finance director or whether he's going to be working in training, and they'll tell you all sorts of things; did he ask questions, did he have an enquiring mind, was he polite to them, did he interact with team members, was he late for team briefs, did he work a full day? I'm amazed sometimes. Very senior appointees go for an experience day and I go along afterwards and ask how was so and so – 'oh he left early for a meeting!'

Of course, the body rejects things that don't fit. I think that one of the biggest responsibilities of management is to look after the corporate DNA and be clear minded about who will benefit the DNA and who will not. The key to sustaining success is protecting your DNA. The bigger you get, the harder it gets.

If you ask people in the business, they will say we're better organized, more committed, more clear about what we're doing today than we were five or six years ago. As we are opening in New York now, we've been challenged by the very things that are important to us, the culture, the people and the DNA; I think it's distance, time and geography that make a difference. We sell bagels in New York, which we don't sell here. We sell more filter coffee. The layout is slightly different so there are some elements that are different, but the basic concept is still the same. If I blindfolded you and landed you in New York, you would be in no doubt as to where you were.

Growth and integrity go together, how to keep growing but do it in the right way

Our senior team have broad retail skills, so they start off as people who are interested in the whole business, not just in their little area. Secondly, all of our management team have been purposely appointed as executive directors first and foremost and then as functional specialists. Over the years we've moved responsibilities around quite a lot. So it's not a case of having a strict functional organization, it's more a case of four or five people all of whom have broad skills sitting round the table and setting common goals and clear levels of responsibility but you can't box them in their responsibilities. For example, you can't say that Morag McCay is just the Marketing Director; she also brings new products to market, she's responsible for the supply chain and purchasing which gives her a very round view. We never write each other memos, we write emails and talk to each other, that's about it. Every Monday morning we sit together as a team and review last week's sales and margin, last week's customer comments and basically any other business, we go round the table and see who's got issues that need to be solved. We don't try and solve them at that meeting, we just highlight them and break up into smaller groups and resolve them. The philosophy is that we all sit round the table on a Monday, we're all responsible for the sales, all responsible for margins and all responsible for customer feedback.

The most important measure in the business is sales. We make a big deal of record sales and breaking them. Every time a shop breaks a record we make a bit of a fuss. Our shop at Victoria Station has just opened and had its first £20,000 week – we've got all the managers' names and we give them a call and say 'well done'. We then look at the business as a whole, broken up by category into mature shops and new shops, broken up by various managers so it's pretty standard, boring stuff but it's important to understand how each shop is doing in terms of sales, transactions and pricing, food cost and labour. We also get a report that shows our customer comments for the week. We go through every single customer comment; we normally end up with about 11 to 15 pages of customer comments. All of those comments are categorized into product issues, service issues, new shops, whatever, and then as a management team we go through all of those. So the focus is sales, marketing and customer feedback during the week, then at the end of the month we have a more detailed Key Performance Indicators pack, where we look at everything from new shop performance to team member turnover.

It's all in the detail. We really don't spend time thinking about strategy except a couple of times a year we make the big decisions, where we are going to expand, what rate of growth we are planning, who the key people are we need to hire. Beyond that it's week-in week-out execution of what we do.

Our goal for the future is to continue doing what we do really well and to do it better than anyone else. We feel a real sense of enthusiasm for building this business. I don't think we'd be invigorated by standing still, but I certainly don't want to grow at the expense of some of the values we think are really important. So growth and integrity go together, how to keep growing but do it in the right way. It sounds trite and anybody can tell you that, but it's easy to say and hard to do.

7

Our view is marketing occurs at the first point you have contact with Pret and so our challenge is not to get customers into our stores but to keep them coming back. Organizations spend a lot of money advertising. We don't do that, we take the money we would have spent on advertising and put it back into the quality of our food and the wages of our people. If we do that we'll keep our customers coming back again and again.

Morag McCay

Marketing Director

In Pret, marketing covers what we sell and why we sell it. In a traditional organization it would be a much narrower definition, but in our business if you're going to maintain the integrity from start to finish – and finish means customer service – then you start with where you source the product from and you end with feedback from customers eating it.

We advertise through our packaging, our shop designs and layouts and the 'Passion facts' about our brand on the walls. We use all the normal marketing materials but the human element is far more important. The recommendation or the positive response that a team member can create is worth so much more than anything you can write down on paper. Seventy-five percent of our customers say they will recommend us and 20 percent say they will consider recommending us, so when you get up to 95 percent of your customers being positive that's a pretty strong form of advertising.

Pret has always had this reputation of listening to people, right from the beginning when our founder's phone number was printed on the carry-out bag; it's still on the bag. We actively encourage feedback, whether it's from the shop, or through the central telephone level. When you have a system which is as energetic and as rapid as ours, getting feedback on the finished product in the marketplace can be as valuable as spending time in advance researching it. So we will put a product out in test shops, watch it very closely, get very quick feedback, then make a decision as to how we progress from there.

One of the biggest challenges for Pret is how we retain, nurture and preserve what we have in this small organization as we get larger. I don't think we have the magic answer, we're going to continue to learn and challenge ourselves as we grow. I still think it does depend on recruiting the right people, I still do believe it depends on instilling the same values and ensuring that you're giving people support and encouraging them. If you stop doing that other things start assuming importance, whether it be financial discussions or product discussions or anything else. If you stop talking about the people and the environment your people work in, and the organizational values and the behaviours that are important, then you risk losing the type of service and consistency of service, which is so important.

The thing that is probably different from any other company I've been in is that a lot of head office people are involved in the customer experience. Whether it's our buddy days spent in the shop or staying in touch with the team that work there or holding our one-to-one meetings in the shops rather than in our office. But that's very much what Pret is like, very grounded in where our customers are, and what our customers see and do and experience.

Launa Williams

Manager, Communications

We believe in the mission statement that we created back about 14 years ago and we still believe in it today. We've changed the wording a tiny bit but it's still our mission today to create handmade natural products. And that's what our team actually do. I've been with the company now for six years and we have never, ever sacrificed the quality of any product because it's very important to us and it reflects in the brand and in everything that we do.

When customers come here for the first time they are very surprised at how polite and professional our teams are and how we go the extra mile for them. If something is wrong, we'll go out of our way to put it right. If customers are not happy with something, we will listen to them. If there is something wrong with one of our products, we'll recall it in every single shop. That's how much we care. That's something I admire a lot about Pret. It's the fact that if we do make a mistake we're not afraid to admit it, we're not afraid to tell all our customers we've got it wrong and we'll wait until we can get it right before we put something back on sale. And we do listen to our customers a lot; we listen a lot to our people as well. There are a lot of important things that make Pret a success today: our people, our culture and what we believe in.

The basic thing we have in operation in our shops is our comment card, it's really clever. They're personalized to each manager that runs the shop. So on each card it will say 'Hi I'm Launa, I'm the general manager for this shop'. Every single shop has a team brief every morning where 15 minutes are spent with the team. We get information and we give information back. We're rewarding and motivating the team, but a very crucial part of the day is where we give this customer feedback to the team. The more we share, be it good news or bad news, the more we can grow as a company. Competition is exciting and tough so we've just got to try and keep consistent. By listening to our customers and listening to our people, we'll always learn and we can keep building. It's great when you can actually sit down with the customer, talk to them and say 'well what do you think about that?' We encourage team members to talk to customers. We have a little term for it, the Pret buzz.

Pret are fantastic motivators; they're very good at giving you rewards and motivating you as an individual. What I have found in Pret, personally, is the more you give, the more you're recognized and that makes you want to give more. For example, we have mystery shoppers every week to

The more we share, be it good news or bad news, the more we can grow as a company come in and snapshot the business. How was your service today, did you smile, did you give eye contact, did you have a great selection, what time did you have a great selection, did the person serving on the till give outstanding service? If, for example, one of our team members gives outstanding service, they will get £50 on-the-spot in cash which is fantastic, and makes you feel brilliant. The shops have incentives as well. For example, if a shop gets the best quality audit or mystery shoppers scores in their area, Pret gives the manager £25 per employee and you can go out and do whatever you want with the team.

Pret is a very young and energetic company who believe strongly in their people and their values and I have felt this has been consistent throughout the time I have been here. The good thing about Pret is that you don't feel bad when you make a mistake. Pret gives you an opportunity to look at what you're not so good at and improve on that, so inside you don't feel 'Oh God, I'm not doing very well'. I actually look forward to coming to work in the mornings and your team can see that, your customers can see that. It always starts from the top. They believe in the same things we do. So it filters through. I'm accountable and I'm responsible and it's important how my team feels. If I've had a bad day, I know the team is going to have a bad day, so I know it's important that I don't have a bad day. Everything I do is reflected.

Once we interview a prospective new hire and they meet the basic criteria, we then set up what we call an 'On Job Experience' day. They work in the kitchen on different benches, and then work in the shop, so they would have the experience to say 'I've worked in Pret, is that what I want to do?' So at least then they're not committed to something they don't want to do. By the same token they've got to impress the team members. Every single person working in the shop would have voted yes or no to employ the individual. If 90 percent of the team say 'yes', they've got the job, if 90 percent say 'no', I've got to go on what they say. If they have been unsuccessful, then we pay them for the day.

Those that have been successful are the lucky ones. Over a period of 10 days they will be trained meticulously in the shop and in the kitchen. They will be assigned a trainer who will be looking after them, working side-by-side with them. The trainer will take them through the steps of everything that happens within the company. A team member has to learn six key points of service and six key points of production. These are the things we look for every day. For example, with service we'd be looking at the style, selection, service, speed, say 'thank you' and 'see you again', these are the six things that a customer will experience when they enter the shop. For production it would be perfect ingredients. We have a chart in the kitchen to make sure that the avocados are the right length and texture. If not, we reject them; it's as simple as that. The tomatoes need to be a certain diameter; the cucumber should be a certain length.

Once they've passed, they will get a little pin to say they've graduated and then they will get a pay increase as well. That's saying already at this early stage you've done really well, keep it up, we're going to look after you. After four weeks of somebody joining the company they have a full appraisal. We sit down with the individual and discuss at an early stage, if everything is all right, is there anything they are not happy with, so we don't leave it until a year later and find out that Joe Bloggs has wanted to do the coffee machine for a whole year and nobody's asked him. After three months they get promoted into a team member star, and after that they've got options. We've got a lot of students who come from Spain or Italy for six months or a year. We have found that they've stayed on and made a career of it, because we've looked after them. Now we've started to offer English lessons, to encourage people to stay.

It takes a lot of motivation to make about 200 sandwiches each day, following the recipe cards that say 'you must put the lettuce in this way, you must put the tomato in this way, you must put this and that sauce on, you must put this amount of chicken on, you must put the seasoning on in this direction'. How do you motivate someone to do that? For me I try and inject fun, honesty and integrity into my job. The way you're perceived by the team is all important. I love this company. They respect who you are and what you do that makes a difference. They've helped me, encouraged me, developed me, motivated me so I can naturally do that for my team who are working with me, not for me. It makes a difference.

There's a lot of reward and recognition in Pret. It's nice when you tell somebody that they're doing a really good job and they're not expecting it, suddenly giving someone a pay rise that they're not expecting at all. You make people feel a million dollars by saying 'you've done a fantastic job today'. I sometimes do something really spontaneous and say 'right let's go and have a coffee in the opposition', and you can share with them that this is the reason why we are working at Pret.

On the day when the company opened it was the day of Princess Diana's wedding and the very first shop was opened and no one came to the shop. So you've got this brand new shop opened and everyone's gone to this wedding. So what do we do? We gave all the sandwiches away! We still do that. At the end of the night, the charity Crisis goes round our London shops and collects leftover sandwiches. At Christmas time 10p from the sales of the Christmas Lunch sandwich that we sell goes towards charity. And if you think about it, that's a lot of sandwiches, a lot of shops. We're giving to charity because we want to. Sharing our success.

It's fantastic that many years ago two guys eating sandwiches thought 'I can't believe we can't get something better'. That's all it took. They believed in it and they followed it through, now they've got a fantastic organization. Two guys who were very passionate about something they believed in. Being passionate in Pret is what it's all about!

TESCO

Every little helps.

8

Tesco is generally regarded as one of the great success stories of retailing. Once identified with the 'pile 'em high' philosophy, a deteriorating retail estate and an undifferentiated offer, it has transformed itself into one of the most innovative and admired businesses.

Its complete focus on its customers is such that the board of directors regularly attend customer panels to understand first hand what they are experiencing. This approach, symbolized in its 'every little helps' slogan, clearly works with group sales of £22.8 billion, profits in excess of £1 billion, a successful expansion into overseas markets and a host of awards for customer service and employee satisfaction. It is also one of the few retailers to have developed a successful online offer.

The Tesco story demonstrates that empowering staff and rewarding them in a way that reflects the mantra 'treat your employees like you would treat your customers' is the bedrock of a great brand experience.

8

Terry Leahy
Chief Executive Officer

When I joined the board of Tesco PLC in 1992, the supermarket industry was experiencing a difficult period. I remember a *Sunday Times* headline around that time announcing the end of the supermarket era. A subheading said it would be toughest for Tesco. Like many media stories, it exaggerated the problem. But what was true was that we, at Tesco, had been so busy benchmarking Sainsbury's that we had lost focus on our own customers. Our research told us we were following, not leading.

It was a defining period and from that day on we changed the philosophy and direction of the business. We decided to follow our own customers, rather than follow everybody else. What immediately followed was a recovery strategy based around a single theme: listening very carefully to customers and responding directly by changing the organization. More recently, we have articulated this as a principle – our core purpose – which is to 'create value for customers, to earn their lifetime loyalty'. This core purpose is on a card which everyone at Tesco carries in their wallets and purses.

Of course, what rapidly becomes apparent in a service business like ours is that you can only look after the customer by looking after your staff. So, the route to creating value for the customers is through the management of your people. Good retailers always understand this instinctively and we, at Tesco, regard it as a major priority.

I spend most of my time with customers and staff. I attend hundreds of customer panels all over the country and I sit at the back and listen. It's a great thing to do and teaches me a lot. You get all your mistakes paraded in front of you – much more immediate than reams of research. The one thing I know will happen every time is that a customer will stand up at some point in the evening and say 'the reason I shop in your store is because of your staff', and that will be greeted with general acclaim. They will never stand up and say 'the reason I shop in your store is because of the prices or the marketing campaign or the advertising or the store design'. It's none of those things. It's always the staff: a constant reminder in a service business of who delivers the experience.

No manager or management team can possibly create that shopping experience for 12 million customers – a quarter of a million staff can. But they will only do it if they believe in the business and believe in what the business stands for. That's the kind of commitment we believe we have generated and which shone through brilliantly in the fuel crisis in the UK in October 2000. It was an extraordinary week for Britain. In a lean economy, you had only hours to keep the country going, so companies like ours had to prioritize. We had plans to help suppliers get products through and plans for customers and so on. But the one group we really didn't have to plan for was our staff. I don't know how they did it, but they got into work. Walking, riding on horses, who knows? But

'Uncommon Practice' at Tesco

Share ownership scheme

Customer panels

Above industry average salaries

Save As You Earn scheme

Retraining programme for 12,000 managers

Day-long seminars for staff to establish values

One-in-front initiative

Above average internal promotions

External and internal value statements

Annual customer plan

they got into work. They didn't need to be given an incentive or be organized in any way. They knew they were needed, that their customers would have a special problem and they were going to battle on through.

To reach such a level of commitment is a long haul. In some ways, it takes a generation. We've had to revolutionize and change completely the way we manage. We have altered pay and benefits in the business out of all recognition. In the past 10 years, there has been a very significant increase in the pay of all our people, paid for by big increases in productivity. We pay them as well as we can, they're paid better than other people and they are very motivated.

More than that, we have introduced a share ownership scheme for 80,000 staff which has an enormous influence on their sense of involvement and ownership of the business. Our Save As You Earn scheme has created something like £400 million of value for our staff in the past five years. In some exceptional circumstances, they actually created more wealth than they received in pay over the same period. For most, it was a very useful addition to their earnings. And it is an important alignment of the interests of the business, the shareholder and the employee.

Our 12,000 managers have taken part in a massive retraining programme over a two-year period. It was principally about teaching them a new toolkit of skills so they can add value to the business, support front-line staff, define people's roles, communicate and plan better, give support and manage teamwork. All of this was designed to make work more satisfying and the workplace more effective. But as well as looking after our people better, we needed to communicate a plan to them, which they could believe in, so we set out certain strategic goals underneath our core purpose. Ours was to be a growth business and we would run it in the right way to earn the loyalty and commitment of our people. We would grow in non-food and be as strong in that area as food. This was a major new departure for Tesco. Another was international growth. All of this signified big, important changes and challenges for the business.

In a watershed move some five years ago, we asked hundreds, possibly thousands, of our staff, split into small groups, what Tesco stood for and what they would like Tesco to stand for. What they were doing in those day-long seminars over a 12-month period was, of course, articulating the values of the business. Having asked the staff their views, we then drew that feedback together, wrote it up in typical management speak and gave it back to our people who then re-wrote it after they said it was unclear and not very engaging. They wrote it in very plain English and now their words have become our values.

These values are about two things: the customer and the way we treat each other – four things we do for the customer and six we do for each other. It's actually our management charter in the business. It's how you manage in any situation; understand the customer; be first with the customer; use your strength to deliver unbeatable value; look after the staff so they can look after the customer; teamwork; trust, respect.

All of the things are in there that describe the culture of the business. They have been a very powerful influence on Tesco. The values give people a clear culture and give young managers a clear sense of what is the right thing to do. I like that phrase. I don't know where it comes from, but when in doubt 'do the right thing'. If you're in a far off country, on your own in a remote place, in a remote department, you don't have a rulebook telling you what to do. But if you instinctively know the right way to treat customers or staff, then you'll do the right thing.

It's even more important to have strong values as you move internationally, particularly in retailing, because much of the value, many of the key decisions, are in the local market. Therefore, it is terribly important that your people make the right decisions, because they have to make them on the ground and they possess a guiding principle in order to make them. Internationally, we have been careful to test the translation of these values into other cultures, other languages. They've gone down pretty well, because they're about how you treat each other, the nature and dignity of work, the nature of service and the dignity of service towards customers. In other words, there is a universal desire for people to enjoy their work and derive satisfaction from helping other people – in this case, customers. This helps enormously in recruitment, not only in terms of attracting people who hold similar values, but in providing a clear message to everyone about what the business stands for.

There is no better example of this than when we were recruiting for graduates in Korea. Our partner there, Samsung, always attracts the top graduates from the Korean universities, as it is regarded as a very reputable employer. Retailing does not have that reputation in Korea, so we could have had some difficulty. But I was pleasantly surprised. Our team simply placed an advert featuring our values; that's all they did. Korean graduates flocked to Tesco, because they had read the values and said 'that's the kind of organization we want to work for'. So, it is very important for recruitment.

All of this has flowed naturally from our initial desire to listen to customers and respond by creating benefits for them through our staff. But then, to ensure the business changed as customers' lives changed, we brought in from all over the world new skills and techniques in order to do it even better. What you're really signing up to with our core purpose is a commitment to change every part of the business in order to stay useful for customers. Even though the industry and food may not grow a lot, people's lives change enormously. Of course, our competitors may well say 'well, we're trying to represent the same thing within our organization'. But our values came from the business itself. They were articulated by the business and based on each individual's experience of how they would like Tesco to be. So, it wasn't brought from outside, out of a management textbook and patched on to the business, and I think that was very important.

What's also important is that you live the values. They have to be central to how you operate the business, the way you manage in order to affect processes and projects, and how people work.

Watch what you do rather than what you say

So grounding, as the Americans say, is terribly important. There's an old phrase 'watch what you do rather than what you say'. So, if I spend my time on customers and on staff, and on the values, that's what the business will concentrate on.

Ultimately, though, it's the board who own this brand and make decisions about it. The brand name travels with us as Tesco moves into other areas like personal finance, the internet and non-food products. It is not a conglomerate of businesses. It's a single business. Similarly, when we open in other countries, it's not always, but usually, called Tesco, so it's important that our business values – our approach to customers and staff – are recognizable. Our business strategy and our brand strategy are almost inseparable, because one so closely defines the other. And it's our job to explain to our owners our strategy for the business and how value is created.

Early on, I remember there was some concern in shareholding institutions about our focus on customers. You occasionally heard the phrase 'Tesco is good for customers, but not good for shareholders'. Very quickly, however, they realized that the best route to long-term value creation for shareholders was by creating benefits for customers and you never hear that concern these days.

And what makes our Tesco people try that bit harder for customers is that they have mainly grown up as underdogs. Often, in their personal lives or in a business context, they've been number two or three. So, they're much better as a group at the bottom of the mountain looking up than they are at the top, looking down. When we became number one retailer in the UK, for example, the best thing we could have done was to expand internationally. Immediately, we slipped down the league table and amongst international players we were number four or five. This has propelled the business forward to scale new peaks.

The day-to-day pressures of competition in a low-growth, highly competitive industry like ours never allow you to feel complacent, though. People work fantastically hard in our industry and in our business, and if you make a mistake, which we often do, you're punished by customers straight away. So you never feel you have some sort of magic formula that predetermines your success and that's important. What you do need is consensus in a business, because that will produce a better outcome. It just does. But you cannot afford to ignore original, independent thought either and you have to listen, be vigilant, outward-looking and be alert.

This needs to be combined with a style that encourages listening internally, too. You can't listen to customers and not listen to staff. It doesn't work that way. So, you have to listen to the voice that says 'I'm not sure we're doing this the right way'. It's evolution, not revolution. Rapid evolution.

8

Treat each other the way you like to be treated

Tim Mason

Director of Corporate Marketing

We have been able to convince customers that we are on their side. We went through a period in the early 1990s when customers said Tesco are in it more for profit than they are for me. We responded to that with a series of initiatives such as, 'One in front', bag packers, and the Clubcard. I think the consumer recognized that we were being innovative because we didn't have to do these things. 'Every little helps', which is our slogan, encapsulates our attitude. We try to create value for customers so that we earn their lifetime loyalty. There is something about the culture here that just makes our people try a little bit harder.

I think the trick may be that the business has always valued 'entrepreneurial spirit'. This company doesn't encourage people to leave their brains at home when they come to work. As a result of that, people have been less of a slave to a system and actually much more responsive to the environment they're in. We are less system-focused than some companies: what you get in Tesco is a lot more people moving a lot higher, above the average than you do in organizations where they follow the system, where they do it by rote. One of the best things we ever did, to move service forward in the business, was to say to people that what we want you to do is treat your customers the way you would like to be treated. We told our managers that is what we want our staff to be able to deliver and, therefore, you've got to manage them in a way that encourages them to do that, enables them to do that and doesn't punish them if they get it wrong. Malcom Gluck, the 'Super Plonk' guy, said something along the lines of 'the people at Tesco are bending over so far backwards to help customers that they must have curvature of the spine!' That is what we want the impression to be, and when you see it and hear it, it's just fantastic. It is around the exceptional. It's around the child who falls over and hurts him or herself and how we respond to that. I always feel if you ever get in a crisis, just get a couple of Tesco managers and a couple of Tesco people around you and they'll sort it out.

We are working hard to communicate the values of the business and they are both external and internal. We headline them into a short, encapsulating statement. The external one is 'no one tries harder for customers' and the internal one is 'treat each other the way you like to be treated'. The thing is continually evolving and developing as much as anything else because it is the nature of human beings to get bored so you have to keep finding ways to reinvent, to rejuvenate and re-energize to keep the spirit of service alive. My view is that within the next five years there will be a new thing that managers will need to do and that will be to make work fun. I think what you'll find is that staff will gravitate towards employers who make work fun. What you'll see is that it becomes a key feature of recruitment and retention, alongside benefits.

It is in our DNA to be more customer-focused. We're quite good at strategic planning but what we're actually really good at is doing things – doing things for customers. We don't talk about it, we do it. Most businesses have plans, some business plans are better than others. Where most businesses fall down is that they don't implement their plans, they implement something that's not their plan but is somebody else's. Fewer layers, less bureaucracy helps. To some extent it's the culture that drives the structure, rather than the structure driving the culture. You facilitate the culture.

One of the things that we also try to do in the business is to be relevant and attractive to relatively small subsets of the population. One of the things you've got to be aware of is that by listening to a statistically selected group of the population, you actually don't hear what the minority group is saying because it's drowned out by the other 97 percent. What we try to do is find the 3 percent, 4 percent, 5 percent and listen to what they're saying because if we can be significantly more appealing to 3 percent more customers, we'll have a very good year.

Now our best customers are not all the same, in fact our best customers are very different, who we try and understand our best customers and do the best job we can for them. You have to walk the talk. The truth of service is that so much of it is actually to do with values, culture, the way in which you go to market. It's terribly difficult to teach and you can only teach it to an amazingly receptive audience.

David Potts

Director of Retail Operations

In many ways the brand is kept alive by having very good store managers. Equally the people who run the business here are close to the business. Directors are in our stores and the rest of the board visit the stores a lot. We therefore find out the issues that are affecting staff and their customers very quickly.

The people we hire have an empathy with people and are interested in their jobs. Our managers have their ears to the ground and are able to talk about the day-to-day business to ordinary people, which in our book makes them extraordinary. They have also got to retain their enthusiasm. It's quite a demanding job, 500 to 600 staff in each store, we're always open, 24 hours a day, seven days a week, we take a lot of money, it's pretty tough. A lot of energy, resilience, enthusiasm and physical fitness is required.

We look for people who enjoy working with people, somebody who is naturally outgoing and social, and is prepared to help people. Many of our jobs are routine and fairly straightforward but the extra bit is the interaction with the customer. There was a great Tesco story in the *Manchester Evening News* recently. A lady from the States was visiting her son who lived in Manchester. She needed a wheelchair to get around and her son saw a wheelchair in the local Tesco and asked if he could borrow it. The store said no because it was the only one they had, but without saying anything else to the man, a store employee, not a manager, got on to another local Tesco which had three wheelchairs, borrowed one of theirs and delivered it to the man's house with a bunch of flowers for his mother. There are so many examples of that where staff and management do what they believe is right so long as it's responding to customers.

Customers expect to be listened to: we have to have the time and attitude and capacity to listen, more importantly, this determination will help our customers respond to what's been said. That goes a long way. We run regular customer question times up and down the UK and publish the results of what customers have said to everyone in the business. The details get distributed to the board, and we all read them very carefully, not really for the store specifics, we're always looking for trends or issues emerging. Customers may start to say I can't reach some products or when I take my trolley in there's always stuff in the way or I had to queue to get out, and that, for us, would say we are putting too much clutter in the store, we're putting the shelving too high or have we lost the plot on service, is it affecting all the stores? We are very energetic in our determination to improve things for the customers continually.

There is a big belief that we're providing value for money in Tesco. We have what we call a 'Customer Plan' every year where, based on research and our own observations and experiences during the year, we define what the emerging issues in Tesco are, what the emerging issues in the country are, etc. Our business strategy more or less lives or dies by the Customer Plan. We spend a lot of money each year on carrying out whatever we put into our Customer Plan. We prioritize our actions on the plan, it's a short list but involves major change. We apply it very determinedly and have sales targets for all of the plans and measure them regularly.

We train our staff to take people to where things are, rather than pointing in the general direction. We take that customer service online too. The staff get to recognize the names of customers and the staff who deliver the goods have a very good relationship with the customer. They often enter their house and it seems to us that you can't get more personal than taking the goods into somebody's house. I often think to myself that we, at Tesco, have got far more to lose with our staff than any other retailer in the UK, because they do far more for our customers than anybody else.

Nowadays we say as long as we've hired the right person, and have broadly explained what we want them to do, they should be allowed to get on and do it. We can have all the good ideas we like but it's the little exchanges that take place in the store between our members of staff and customers that actually make the difference. The customers recognize the staff make a difference. Staff have got to believe that the leadership is interested in the business and understands and values the things they want to do, but their relationship with the customers is our future.

easyGroup

Stelios Haji-Ioannou founded easyJet with a £5 million loan from his father. It soon became one of the most admired airlines in Europe, a successful low-cost operator, which was one of the few brands to exploit successfully the direct channel that the internet provided.

A combination of an award-winning approach to customer service, a unique business culture and an idiosyncratic, high-profile approach to publicity turned easy into a strong brand that could straddle a number of markets. easyEverything, easy.com, easyRentacar and easyMoney have followed and the easyGroup is now widely regarded as one of the success stories of recent years. The root of this continuing success is in the culture that easyGroup encourages: a non-hierarchical, truly open culture where knowledge is power!

9

Stelios Haji-Ioannou

Chief Executive Officer, easyGroup

If I am honest with myself, I have to admit that I did not start a brand. I started an airline, which became a brand. Back in '94/'95 when I decided to invest in the airline business, I started my research. I wasn't a marketing professional, I didn't have any formal training. I came from the shipping industry, which is the ultimate unbranded business. I started understanding what a brand is and how companies position themselves. In deciding the brand for the airline, the positioning, the advertising, the marketing and everything else, I had a role model. I was always fascinated by, and had always been a customer of, Virgin Atlantic but I very quickly realized it would not be a profitable strategy for the short-haul business, that's not where the gap in the European market is. So I went to the States and followed very closely a company called Southwest Airlines.

Southwest Airlines is probably the epitome of delivering brand through people. I came back with these ideas and said if we're going to have a chance of surviving in this war, winning this battle, we've got to develop a culture, a personality and we've got to position this airline as something different to BA and British Midland and every other airline which flies short haul around Europe. I stayed well clear of my personal preferences and likes and dislikes. I said that is not relevant, we have to develop a different personality.

The first thing I did was walk the talk; I took my tie off, started dressing down. I worked from an office in Luton. All of that was part of a plan to create a culture which keeps costs down. At the end of the day, branding is not only for the customers but also for the employees. You send a very strong message if you say to people that we don't have plush offices. We dress down. That's how we can offer low fares. Firstly it's cheaper in the sense that people who dress up and wear ties and suits usually expect big offices and an army of secretaries outside to fulfil every dream and wish. It's a more egalitarian approach to office management and management style that says you shouldn't really be able to tell who the boss is and who is working for whom. We're all together in this. I said this company would be different, open plan, open culture, nothing to hide. We share information, we have no taboos, no secrets, everything is paperless – that became our internal culture.

I was very keen to give as many reasons as possible to our customers to explain why we are so cheap because in starting an airline there's always a safety question mark hanging over your head. When you say to people you can fly to Scotland for £29, they say 'it can't be done, there must be something wrong with this plane, it's unsafe'. I was very keen from the beginning to keep hammering home why we're cheaper. A lot of the brand culture has developed out of that desire and the need to remind customers how it is we are able to achieve these low fares. It's not because we don't maintain the engines, we developed a crusade to cut out the middle man and developed a direct channel to the consumer. It was a very neat way of explaining to customers why we are cheaper; it is because you buy direct.

'Uncommon Practice' at easyGroup

Dress-down style for everybody

---

10 percent of the easyJet equity is set aside for stock options for staff

---

Culture of keeping costs down

Open plan, open culture, nothing to hide

Culture committees in each company

Paperless office

Friday afternoon get-togethers for staff

Big staff parties in the summer and at Christmas

Total transparency – everyone has access to company performance data

---

The need to communicate directly to our customers created another need in the company and that is to be high profile, brash and 'in your face' because you can't be quiet and reticent and expect customers to find your phone number and look for you. We don't have travel agents pushing our product. We really have to be loud, so that developed, almost by necessity, another attribute of easyJet which is to be brash.

The brand developed by necessity. If we didn't make brash, loud, orange advertising, people wouldn't notice us. A brand doesn't exist on a designer's board, I think it really exists in the minds of the consumers, so that's how I designed it.

I'm a guy who likes to start companies, I don't like running big companies. I built a shipping company, I built an airline, I'm now building a chain of internet cafés, a rent-a-car company and a couple of other crazy ideas. The point is that I very quickly realized that unless I was going to stay and run the airline on a day-to-day basis, which I didn't want to, I would run out of things to do. Because I wasn't ready to retire, I invented this concept of brand extension. Again, I looked at Virgin and I hired a few people around me to form this company which we call easyGroup. This is an incubator to start new ideas. When we first came up with an idea the question came up about what we were going to call it. I said I think we should do brand extensions and call all the companies 'easy'. There is something about brand extension that captures customers' imagination. It's much more powerful than a company spending money to advertise itself. To use an airline and then suddenly see a coffee shop which looks the same, and has some of the same characteristics, but with a different purpose, then to see the same brand applied to a car, then to internet shopping and banking and so on is very powerful.

I said let's define a list of characteristics that an 'easy' company should have. Firstly, we only look at opportunities that can actually become PLCs one day. We only look at things that are value for money, we're not at the luxury end of the market. We believe that we should be able to significantly re-engineer a product because price is a function of cost. Unless you can re-engineer the cost, you can't be competitive. I would not get into the car rental business just to offer a car like everyone else. I would get into the car rental business because I identify sustainable, competitive advantage.

Another 'easy' principle is we don't want to be all things to all men. We choose our target audiences and go for them. For instance, I find booking online highly convenient, I know some people who hate it and will never do it. For them we are a nuisance because they can't rent our cars. We've excluded 50 percent of the population by virtue of the way we rent our cars. So we design the product for the target audience. We don't say 'how do I make sure that everyone has access?'.

Either by accident or design, every single business that we're in is a service business. We sell a service, so our people are very, very important. Developing a culture amongst the employees has always been a high priority in all my companies. It's achieved over time. It is naïve, if not pretentious, to say you can have a culture from day one. When we go out to recruit people to start a company, these people do not have our culture and we need to instil it, to make them 'orange'.

It takes time and effort and it takes a battle. There's nothing like a good crisis or competitive battle to give a group of people a team spirit. We are also big on parties and encourage people to socialize with each other. We sponsor Friday afternoon get-togethers within the company and we have big parties at Christmas time and in the summer. We inject fun.

We now have 2,500 staff and I've discovered that although the company gets bigger and you lose some of that small team spirit, people are actually more proud to work for a well known, bigger company that's successful that everybody at home and in their neighbourhood talks about. You sustain some of that enthusiasm through other ways, for example, through stock options. I set aside 10 percent of the equity of easyJet for staff.

I always believe that every company should be above the shop, figuratively speaking. easyEverything, our internet café company, is above one of the shops and easyRentacar, when it's big enough to move out of head office, will move above one of the car parks. In head office I believe we should all muck in and understand what the rest of the company is all about. I communicate to people with emails a lot and encourage them to be open. All our reports are distributed to everybody. We encourage head office people to get themselves out on to the front line. There's nothing better for managers than being at the 'coal face'.

One of the other things I do is to hold meetings standing up. It conveys a sense of urgency. They always last less time and people get straight to the point, it keeps them on their toes and people understand that there is a problem to be solved.

The way I measure performance is to talk to customers. I talk to staff as well, but if I really want to find out what's happening in the business I talk to customers. My early warning radar is customers, not employees. On easyJet it's very easy. I get on a plane, fly, walk up and down the aisle and ask them. One of the benefits about being relatively famous in the UK is that people recognize me and talk to me. They complain, they praise, they thank, whatever. I was in easyEverything today, I sat down and was checking emails within the store specifically to make myself available, and the guy next door looked up and recognized me and said 'well done for this business. I use it all the time'. If you make yourself available to customers and you have the face recognition, then sooner or later people will speak to you. If you build a brand around a person, then you always have a risk of something happening to that person be it either physical or reputation. I think it's the downside that generally comes with every up side. If you want a faceless organization, then you don't do it but you won't achieve the same level of brand awareness.

We have a lot of customer data. I was looking at numbers today for easyEverything – it's just mind-blowing the amount of data we have. We know what customers do, how long they stay, how many times they purchase a ticket. It's amazing that even in places where the brand is relatively

Brand extensions

easyGroup
_____

easyJet
_____

easyRentacar
_____

easyEverything
_____

easyMoney
_____

easyValue
_____

easy.com
_____

young and the product is young, like easyRentacar in Paris, the regular repeat business, which we define as someone who has booked a car with us before, is up to 50 percent. For me that means loyalty. Repeat business is really the only measure of loyalty I'm looking for. You know what repeat business tells you more than anything else? That the product is acceptable. That you've found a target audience, a customer base, that finds the product so good that they're willing to use the product again and again. Because I deconstruct businesses and eliminate waste, there is a risk that I will go too far. I think the CEO of Continental said you can always make pizza with less cheese but if you remove all the cheese it's not called pizza any more! One useful gauge of whether you've gone too far is repeat business. If people come back again and again, you know you've pitched it right.

I've been asked what sort of advice to give to anybody else on how to build such a brand other than being adopted by a rich father! Actually, it's only partly a joke. I had the capital to start an airline and to take on BA and that's what started the business. It's not my ability to design white letters on an orange background that created the brand. But my real advice would be: don't start by designing a brand, start by designing a product and then find a brand that suits it. One of the things I found amusing with the dotcom bubble was that people were looking for shortcuts to creating a brand. You can spend £15 million on advertising, go bankrupt and your name can still mean nothing to people. Your brand is created out of customer contact and the experience your customers have of you.

Ray Webster

Chief Executive Officer, easyJet

Over time we realized that the difference between a good airline and an indifferent airline is the people. Even when we were very small we put emphasis on making sure all of our staff understood the business and had the right attitude. Fundamentally it's very difficult to change your attitude, so hiring attitude as well as on-the-job training and leadership, as an example of the culture, are critical. On the other side of the coin, you need to have people who have the right attitude who can live up to the values, whilst not compromising on all the must-have qualities such as reliability, accountability, etc.

We also put a lot of effort into building good management information systems, ie, sharing information with all staff. We have the belief that by doing this we can add another dimension to all individual employees. By sharing, everyone feels responsible for the business. Part of our culture is that we can't hide. We're all part of the same operation. So there are no secretaries, everybody is on first-name terms, we have an open-plan office. It's a collegiate environment. To build a strong service brand you first need to have an offer that people really want, and only then can you build a brand around it.

9

James Rothnie

Director of Corporate Affairs, easyGroup

You first need to have an offer that people really want, and only then can you build a brand around it

We allow market forces to establish the price, in a way that the consumer should be able to understand. The really important thing about the easyGroup of companies is that we tend to underpromise and overdeliver. We don't compromise on the hardware. easyJet flies a uniform fleet of brand new Boeing 737s. easyRentacar operates a uniform fleet of brand new Mercedes A-class cars. easyEverything uniformly offers brand new Hewlett Packard computers. So you may not get somebody giving you a 'free' glass of champagne or leather seats or whatever, it's a fairly sparse no-frills environment in which we just concentrate on the hardware. New planes, new cars, new computers.

We hire for attitude rather than skills. You need to be somebody who thrives in an open-planned environment, who doesn't need their own private office, who doesn't want to wear a suit and a tie particularly. Somebody who can muck in with everybody. And the other important thing to mention here is that, once you're in the company, we share information. Minutes of the board meeting, financial plans, salaries of your colleagues, it's all there in the system.

Any press release we send out, I automatically copy everybody, the entire mailing list, so they know what's going on. I've got a press monitoring agency who can web stream me the TV, press and radio clips, again, I copy them to the whole office. If somebody does an interview in easyRentacar, then someone in easyValue is more than welcome to listen to it. I just send it round with an email saying this is where you can find it, go ahead and listen if you want.

Knowledge is empowerment. An employee who is given all knowledge really feels like they're part of the company and helping to run the company. And it makes you a more productive employee because you know more and can get things done and shift information around, tell people what's going on and they can give you feedback. You have to be careful to try not to dictate too much from on high and check that the strategy you're trying to develop is logistically and operationally possible on ground level too.

Each company has its own culture committee. It's a representative, elected by their own departments, to come and represent that area on the culture committee. It's a way of making sure we have the right working conditions and we're maintaining the right atmosphere and projecting ourselves correctly across the company. It's a sort of internal brand exercise. Is management appearing in the right way to people working on the shop floor? Is the shop floor appearing in the right way to management? It's an informal way of helping to run the business, more on a cultural level than on a strategic level.

Chris Goscombe

Head of People Development, easyJet

We have a model which operates on two triangles. The first triangle is about the low-cost airline traveller, which means we need to have low costs and be operationally good so we can offer low fares. The challenge is that whilst that looks like a complete winner, it is virtually unsustainable because in this model you could be incredibly late and unsafe, so you need to have another level on top of this, which is to have incredibly high quality relating to safety and a brilliant service, and what you end up with is these two paradoxes. You offer a really low cost and are able to deliver at a very high standard. You're expecting people to deliver a service which is in keeping with low. Because those people drive that paradox. And that's really what the culture is: it's very hard work.

We're not training people to do things a certain way. The training is getting people to appreciate the nature of relationships, of teamwork, and giving the people confidence to step into that environment and deliver with it. It's not that we tell them exactly what to do.

We have five values that go with that. First of all we have 'lean and mean', which is about teamwork and the way in which individuals work together. Being 'up for it' is about how we behave, being able to step into a challenge and work effectively with people. 'Sharp', which is really about listening and understanding, keeping your ear to the ground, understanding what's really going on and great ideas around that, which encapsulates quality, safety, low cost, etc. The next one is 'passion'. I think the way I describe it is that passion is being very enthusiastic, about easyJet obviously, it's about demonstrating it enthusiastically, but when it's going wrong it's also giving people permission to be angry. So it's the whole range of being passionate. The last one is 'pushing boundaries', which is pushing in the sense of being brave with ideas, not being afraid to speak out. To bring these values alive, the process starts before people have even got here, to be quite honest, we select people for their values and attitudes.

I think my final comment is that this is really difficult stuff. It goes wrong, it breaks your heart, it makes you cross. So the idea that this is simple stuff and obvious is just not true. It's incredibly hard to actually do, to achieve a brilliant service consistently. Remember it's not just something you can copy from a textbook, it's got to be real.

10

Few organizations have 3,000 customers eagerly waiting in line for a new store opening. Krispy Kreme does on a regular basis. This US-based manufacturer and retailer doesn't just sell doughnuts – it sells 'magic moments'. From the production line that is on display in every store, to the neon sign that illuminates 'Hot' when a new batch is ready, to the smell of fresh baking that is pumped into the street, the Krispy Kreme brand proposition is all about a multisensory experience. The organization uses retail theatre to create a customer experience in its 200 stores, resulting in a hugely loyal group of customers who are passionate advocates of the brand.

Krispy Kreme epitomizes the concept of the 'Branded Customer Experience®'. By intentionally engaging the senses of customers at every touch-point, it has created a unique customer experience that no competitor can duplicate.

10

Scott Livengood

Chairman, Chief Executive Officer and President

The way we talk about the brand promise internally is that our goal is to create magic moments for our customers, and we view the experience of a Krispy Kreme store as the defining element of the brand. We see the experience of the store as a multisensory experience.

When we began planning to grow Krispy Kreme, we started by going through a process of making sure we fully understood the brand. We are very fortunate that we already have a unique and strong brand. A lot of companies that are just starting out hold planning sessions with their advertising and marketing people to determine what kind of a brand promise they want to create. 'What is the image of the company?' 'How do we want to be experienced?' Often, a brand's image is created to drive marketing and advertising. I felt from the beginning that it was and is crucial to understand the touch points we have with our customer. We distilled the essence of the brand by understanding what our customers really love most about Krispy Kreme. We used that as a platform for what we decided to develop.

I heard things along the way that let me know pretty clearly that we were dealing with something that transcended the opportunity other brands have. One of those occurred when we tore down our store here in Winston-Salem and built another store on the same site. The outcry from the public was startling at first but became a very significant reference point for us. I think that was one of the defining moments for me in understanding the real emotional connection that we have with our customer.

We're immersed in this brand. A lot of us have been around this company for years and we have to be careful not to be overly influenced by our own preconceived notions or ideas. When people find out that you are with the company, they almost invariably have a story. They talk about their experiences as a child with their parent or grandparent, how it involved the store, their impression of the company, the business, and the brand. Understanding Krispy Kreme was a matter of listening to our customers talk about what they most appreciated and what they really loved.

What we tried to do was distil the most loved aspects of the Krispy Kreme experience and then try to do them better, do them more, and do them more authentically; those became our priorities. The most fundamental example I can give you is our stores. The business model up until the '90s was a huge production plant with a small retail area in the front.

A vast majority of the sales – 70-plus, even in some cases 90 percent of sales – were wholesale. Even in those stores, a glass wall gave you a little view of the production process. The view was the very end of the process when the doughnut starts up the conveyor – a cooling conveyor would go around the full perimeter of the top of the building so the doughnuts could cool and come down the other side firm enough to pack in boxes for wholesale distribution.

'Uncommon Practice' at Krispy Kreme

Committed to investing in state-of-the-art training

Annual incentive plan based on customer-service objectives

Quarterly video for employees

Company newsletter

Group meetings once or twice a year

Staff empowered to give free samples

Mystery shoppers and staff use digital cameras to maintain quality

Internal inspections

External surveys

All stores contribute 1 percent of sales to a brand fund

Customers would talk about how they just loved coming to the store when there were hot doughnuts. They'd tell us, 'I came with my grandparents and we saw that the doughnuts were hot, so we came in'. The interesting thing about that was you could barely see the doughnuts being made. The only part you could see was the doughnuts going up a conveyor and cooling. And, the doughnuts were only made hot when it worked best for the wholesale production schedule, because we staged our production schedule so that the doughnuts could be packed fresh for the wholesale market. The trucks usually left between 3:00 and 7:00 in the morning, so most of the production began at 10:00 or 11:00 at night.

We did two fundamental things in reconcepting the company – actually, it was not reconcepting, it was just becoming more of who we are. First, we rebuilt and redesigned the store, put the production equipment right in the middle of the store with a glass wall where you can see the entire production process. Second, we had our hot doughnut production schedule coincide with our highest potential retail periods. We have guaranteed hot hours between 6:00 and 10:00 in the morning and 6:00 and 10:00 in the evening. All our stores should have hot doughnuts during at least those hours, with many expanding beyond those times.

The experience in the store is a magic moment. Customers are able to come in and see, almost literally, magic. Eighty percent of our doughnuts are yeast raised as opposed to many other doughnut stores, which primarily sell cake doughnuts. Our doughnuts are extruded and then pass through a proof box. You can see these little teeny doughnuts get bigger as they proceed through the proof box; they rise just like yeast bread rises. There's magic to that, especially if you're a kid. The doughnuts are little at the start, they are big at the end, and they go through this transformation from white dough to gold – cooked to a golden finish. Then, finally they go through a glaze. It's like the curtain going up as they come out.

We empower our folks to give free samples. Although in a lot of ways we're a manufacturing plant, we're not making automobiles. We can give away a hot glazed doughnut – if there's a long wait for example, or there's somebody who we hear has never had a hot doughnut. Our folks are empowered individually to make those decisions and to respond to things that customers want.

Training is an area that we have begun to grow and to grow more quickly in the last few years. We've made a philosophical and economic commitment to state-of-the-art training in ways that are meaningful and comprehensible to our employees. Our training programme is very experiential and very multisensory. We've realized that traditional printed words and linear training mechanisms don't fully express what our brand is about. We feel that whether it's about equipment or whether it's about customer-service training, we need to have a lot of video and a highly interactive approach.

Instead of a customer-service department, we developed and implemented a customer-experience group. Instead of looking at quantitative sales measures, we established measures through mystery shoppers and our own internal inspections as well as solicitation of off-premises customers through

10

Understanding the customer is our primary marketing imperative

internal surveys. We are receiving information all the time. We try to bring it to a level where we have a great deal of confidence in the information.

We don't just get externally generated data. We use internally generated data so that we can benchmark the sources against each other to make sure we have a high level of confidence in the data. My experience is that when information is all quantitative, all externally generated, like mystery shoppers, there are issues. If enough quality control issues come up, those kind of instruments can lose credibility or not gain the kind of credibility they have to have to mobilize people to action. By having internally generated inspections and store visits – instead of just written reports, we gave digital cameras to all of the folks around the country that do these inspections – everything is supported with a photograph. When we talk to store managers about a problem with quality, something like not enough filling in the doughnut, we have a photograph of the actual doughnut cut open to show the inadequate filling.

To me, understanding the customer is our primary marketing imperative. We have a 1 percent of sales brand fund that all of our stores, company or franchise, are required to contribute to, according to their franchise agreement. In most companies that fund is an advertising fund and goes into traditional media advertising. We call it a brand fund, because to me it's about how we increase our potential. The best way we can increase sales and increase our potential over the long term is to fully understand how we connect with the customer and, on an emotional level, what our customers' expectations are – all the things that got us to where we are now.

It starts with our annual strategic planning process. Starting with the brand promise and the vision that we have, we are obsessive about all of the philosophical issues that define what the brand is about, what our management style is about, how we view each other, and how we see each other's responsibility to everybody else. Ensuring that it is a part of the culture is my responsibility. Everybody in the company, starting with me, is on an annual incentive plan based around customer-service objectives.

The brand touches virtually everything I do, from how I prioritize my time to how I write my letter to the shareholders. If you look at our annual reports, especially the last two or three years, as we have refined those philosophies, I hope you would find consistency in those messages. Any time there is a communication, and we look for opportunities to communicate, there is an intentional reinforcement of our brand values. We communicate by video to our employees quarterly, because again, something like a printed newsletter – which we have – doesn't fully express what's happening with our company and our brand. We reinforce it with video that communicates the experiences that we're having in a way that people will really take in.

Both marketing and sales are organized by channels of sales, as opposed to product line, because the channels of sales are inherently about the customer experience, how a customer experiences Krispy Kreme at each channel, whether it's on-premises or off-premises. The main priorities of both our marketing people and sales people are: how do we add value to each channel we're in and what are the new channels that will increase our potential as a brand?

We're fortunate that we have such a loved brand. We get so much publicity, we have such exciting store openings, and there are so many Krispy Kreme stories and we share these things with everybody in our company. As a result, our back-office folks have the kind of pride and excitement, even if it's vicarious, that everybody else has. We'll have group meetings at least once or twice a year, pull everybody together and share experiences of things that have occurred in the past year and show videos and such. There are many opportunities and tools that we have just because of how well the company is experienced by everybody. It's easy to get everybody passionate about what's going on. There is a respect for the folks out in the field making these things happen that all these people, including the back-office employees, really want to support.

I want to add value to the customer experience, and I want to be able to meet the financial expectations that people have of us. We need to do things that are consistent with both of those objectives. We have to be very careful and part of that is doing market research and understanding things like what price points do not alienate the customer and what are product line additions or product line enhancements that we can bring to the store to add excitement and freshness to the customer's experience.

I have found the most important thing to do is decide what you're about, decide who you are, what you hold as important, and what you value. Make sure that whatever you're doing is about becoming more of what you really are and not about plans and strategies that have financial gain as the starting point. That doesn't mean you can't have aggressive goals. It does mean that you're in for the long run and when times get difficult you have a place to come back to and reaffirm who you are and what you're about; it gives you comfort and confidence in the tough times.

Jack McAleer

Vice-Chairman and Executive Vice-President, Concept Development

Our product, as it relates to brand, is quality. I think that's because of the experience that happens in the store, the emotional connection that people have with Krispy Kreme. It takes the experience and the meaning of quality to a much deeper level, a personal experience. And I'm not sure it happens in many other companies or with many other products. That's why people relate to it. It's more than a brand. It's something that is living in them. I spend time just reflecting on what it is that is so meaningful to our customer in the store environment and makes people walk in and say, 'of course, this is Krispy Kreme'. What are those things that make the magic happen? From the beginning, it's been the theatre, the doughnut theatre and the idea that we're opening up our kitchen, showing the freshness of our product, the process of what is happening and the fact that we're Krispy clean. There is magic there!

We've always encouraged kids of all ages to press their nose against the glass. The doughnut display is in the front of the store. We've always displayed our doughnut jewels right front and centre, with full visibility of the product. We want our customers to be able to choose the doughnut they want, hand picking it if they choose to. 'I want that one with vanilla icing'. Providing the customer with face-to-face contact with the doughnuts right there is central. We're fulfilling that emotional connection by providing them with the end result, which is the bite into the doughnut, the full experience.

Because of the caring nature of our employees, we've always looked at giving our customers a good experience in a 'down home' way. We don't want to be a national company. We always want to maintain our local presence and encourage our employees to do things that help create a better experience. For example, to recognize a birthday, offer a sample, or make sure that a first-time customer gets a hot doughnut. Those kinds of things are extraordinary as they relate to the customer experience. You don't go to other places and see employees, without asking permission, offer something free or take you over to the side and explain what is happening behind the glass when there is an opportunity to do that. So the store – the hot theatre, the hot signs on display, and our employees – complete the experience that pulls the package all together.

The brand has experienced a rapid explosion in the last three years and we have been getting increased awareness out there. It's a magical time here at Krispy Kreme. Everyone is energized by that. Within the organization, there's a great sense of pride about being involved here, wanting to do more, to do it better and give more people the opportunity to have the experience. That's greatly enhanced how we work. In my years here at Krispy Kreme, there's always been a sense of getting the job done, teamwork, across all departments. There's always been the effort to pull together and make whatever it is that needs to happen, happen.

It's quite an experience to be at an opening; to be the one handing out the hot doughnuts, to hear the stories, and to listen to the people interact with each other. It's like a club. Even if they haven't had it before, they very quickly understand something special is happening here. It's common to see a two-hour wait for doughnuts. They get caught up in what's going on. Let me describe what happens. You meet eye-to-eye with a customer and you say, 'is this your first visit to Krispy Kreme?' They say, 'Yes'. We then reply, 'Well, this is our signature product, the Original Glazed doughnut and it's hot'. So they get a doughnut. You wait for them to experience it. And you see one of three things happen, or maybe all three. Their knees bend and then their eyes close. And then, they try to articulate what just happened and say 'Wow'.

Then you continue to tell them, 'This is our signature product. If you look in the window at the "Hot" sign and the red neon is on, it means the doughnuts are coming now'. They look at it to make sure they understand it. Many times somebody behind them or the third person back might say, 'I know' and we then ask that customer to explain what it means and what's happening. So they then tell the story for you. You involve them. You interact with them. You bring it all together

Great brands are experienced

and let them do it for you. It's important to capture events for our entire family to see. We use videos, for example, to share store openings. I think we need to do more there. We're talking to some companies now about being able to play live openings in all of our stores via satellite hookup. Can you imagine all of our employees in all of our stores being able to participate in an opening?

We want to be the world's most-loved brand. Everybody understands that. We're moving in that direction, one customer at a time and one experience at a time and one store opening at a time. That's truly what it's all about. It's just that we're not in any huge hurry to get there. There obviously are challenges about being public and meeting the numbers. But we are very fortunate in being able to touch customers in a way that we get them for a lifetime.

Stan Parker

Senior Vice-President, Marketing

We have identified five key drivers for the brand or customer experience. First is the store experience; second is what we call relationship marketing; third is public relations; fourth is sales promotion; and fifth is advertising. We're involved in all those, but certainly the store is where most of the magic happens. Employees greet you with a friendly smile and know you if you're a regular. The store is where we interact one-on-one with our customers. Customers value the quality of the product, the hot doughnuts specifically. I think customers also value the selection, the variety that we have to offer. Customers also value the store environment. People always talk about the doughnut theatre as something that is really cool and fun to watch; a great experience. Now, we are also starting to hear people talk about how they can trust the product from a safety perspective because of being able to see it made. It gives a sense of comfort in addition to entertainment.

The company culture can be described as 'can do'. The work ethic is tremendous and our people take a lot of pride in doing whatever it takes to get the job done properly. When we receive a customer complaint, we route it to the store manager very quickly, and he or she is expected to follow up with the person who made the complaint. We don't try to resolve it here at corporate. We try to resolve a problem where it's happening. If you had a problem with the store on Ponce de Leon Avenue in Atlanta, you should expect to get a call from the manager of that store to make it right, whatever that might be. Our store managers are empowered.

A great brand transcends product attributes and makes an emotional connection with people. Great brands are experienced. You have to connect with people in a way that is meaningful to them and different from what everyone else is doing. The people in our stores are making it happen and establishing relationships with our customers through the products they are making and the service they are providing. You have to have people in the store who understand the product and how to make it. You have to have people who treat customers right when they come in. A lot of the emails we receive are from customers complimenting our people in the store. Our people are absolutely critical to creating magic moments for our customers. People like to be on a winning team and a part of something that makes other people happy.

Steve Anderson

Director, Customer Experience

In my view, we really began to thrive and think outside the box when we started talking about ourselves as a brand as opposed to a doughnut company. The customers expressed to us that we were a brand before we expressed it to them. That's when the experience began to be tied to the brand, and we began to talk about things other than doughnuts. Now, we describe our experience as people, product and place, whereas seven years ago, we were a doughnut company. The brand, itself, has created certain visions and promises in customers' own minds, not something we've articulated in advertising. I think it's all experiential – customers experience certain things in our store – and that, in essence, becomes the brand promise.

Initially, this department was set up as a customer-service department, and it was Scott who changed it to 'Customer Experience Department'. That was when he really chose to begin the process of educating and introducing the rest of us to branding. It's been a hard road, because we are so operationally oriented. I've tried to make a difference with new store managers. I have access to them through the training when I do a session on the customer experience. Their expectation is typically that we're going to talk about smiling, greeting, thanking customers and that kind of thing. I never talk about that. What I talk about is finding people. I talk about recruiting. I talk about interviewing. I talk about how a person fits in.

Our brand is communicated through stories. We have a stories box on our website where customers will tell their Krispy Kreme story. We don't advertise primarily because many of our customers would be offended by it. The way we open a new store is through PR; it's not through advertising. We carried 5,000 doughnuts into Oklahoma City and we let the doughnuts and delivery folks talk for us. 'Hi, I'm from Krispy Kreme. Here's a doughnut, enjoy it'. So customers are already having an experience. And then they're lining up 24 hours in advance to get into a company that, seven years ago, had very low self-esteem. All of a sudden in the last two, three years, we have figured out that our customers understand us better than we do. Let's go learn from them. And let's allow them to tell their stories and let them communicate. That's how our brand is communicated.

My favourite customer-experience story was watching the production person up front at the glazer stirring the glaze up, because it has to be done every now and then. There was a kid looking in at him, watching him do that. He just looked up and waved at this kid. The kid just went bananas. He ran to his mom and said, 'Mommy, mommy he waved at me'. The kid had a magic moment, and the mom had a magic moment because her kid was pleased. The guy that was stirring the glaze had a magic moment because he realized the impact of his action – all he's done is wave. I had a magic moment, because I saw the whole thing. Four people had a magic moment. It was not orchestrated and it wasn't in the training manual.

Barbara Thornton

Vice-President, Human Resources

We are in the business of creating magic moments through people, place and product. That holds a huge amount of guidance for my department, in finding the people who can create those magic moments for our customers. Also, it guides us in creating magic moments for our internal population. The challenge is finding the right people who can become passionate about Krispy Kreme, who can share that passion through their work and with their customers, and who are interested in growing with Krispy Kreme. The other challenge is helping people currently within the organization to understand the passion for the brand and to help them see this company as it is now.

To be totally truthful, it's constant work to align our people, projects, our programmes and our systems to that ultimate objective of being sure that we are creating magic moments. We designed revised training programmes specifically to engage new employees in the passion around the brand and the culture. We completed the revision on our management training programme and we are in a test phase, currently, with our hourly training programme. What we tried to do is to connect the employee, in a very special way, to the company. Given that we are spread out geographically, that connection can be difficult to achieve. The experience with Krispy Kreme, depending on the store manager, the franchise owner or the company leadership, could be very different at different locations so we tried to provide consistency and a commitment with the brand as a whole through our new training programmes. The programmes have been developed with a multimedia approach incorporating on-the-job training, workbooks, video and computer-based training.

first direct ◀▶

Member HSBC *Group*

11

First Direct single-handedly redefined the retail banking industry in the UK by being the first bank to offer 24-hour banking direct by telephone, a service that has since been expanded to internet banking and mobile phone banking.

A business which has its customer-focused brand at the centre of its internal and external culture, customer loyalty is such that it is recommended by its customers every five seconds and over a third of customers join through personal recommendation. This amazing customer loyalty has been achieved by creating totally new operational processes to support its strategy and new products to meet the individual needs of its highly targeted customers. With over 4,000 employees, it has a dynamic, fun and non-hierarchical culture, which puts a high emphasis on attitude. In order to reinforce the importance of the individuality of the customer, it seeks to do the same with its people – employees are offered a package of benefits that enables the individual to tailor their particular remuneration to their stage in life.

Peter Simpson

Commercial Director

First Direct is like the British constitution in that we've never really written down what it's about. Whether that's a strength or a weakness I'm not sure. We see ourselves as doing two things: one is making people feel better about their interfaces with financial institutions; the second is to make people better off. It's what you actually do which enables you to talk about these things. That's what the brand is really about.

I've always felt that the organization does two things. It's about an ethos we believe in, which some people call culture; and it's also about knowledge. We would describe First Direct as an amoeba-shaped organism, with a centre and nucleus. The centre is half culture and half knowledge, and everything else is systems and all that sort of stuff. The brand really is the way in which you integrate knowledge and culture. Lots of organizations are working very hard on their culture and values, and you see lots of organizations working very hard on their customer-relationship management. I think trying to do both of those in isolation is not going to get the company anywhere. The thing we got right was understanding that integration of the two is what leads to success.

What First Direct did was to realize that people were changing their habits and would want to bank 24 hours a day, seven days a week. The way to do that was to have telephone distribution and a centralized, low-cost manufacturing or processing system. So that's what we put together and we ended up with a large warehouse (three actually), which now holds 4,000 people, for telephone distribution. That was the insight – people would change their banking habits as a way of satisfying their needs. I think that all great brands have insight.

Our competitors found it hard to understand, for some time, that a face-to-face relationship isn't necessarily as strong as one over the telephone if the one on the telephone interface has got vastly superior knowledge. You can have a nice conversation about your financial affairs but unless I know all your previous conversations with us, and what your real aims in life are and what you've said to us in the past, no amount of good conversation between us is going to help much. I think the paradox of First Direct was that we were able to provide better service on the telephone than our competitors were providing face-to-face in branches. We believed that for a good five years, so we had a five-year advantage in doing that. We've extended that paradox, because we then said 'I bet we can have a better conversation on screen than we can on the telephone' and we're in the middle of proving that at the moment. It looks as if it's possible, again because the amount of information you can present on screen is greater than the information you can present over the telephone. Therefore the knowledge side of the relationship increases and whilst the rapport on screen isn't as great as it could be in conversation, the combination of knowledge and rapport can lead to a better interaction than is possible over the telephone. The nature of the interaction

'Uncommon Practice' at First Direct

Internal brand values are
identical to external brand values

Non-hierarchical organization

Events twice a year where CEO
talks to all the employees

Brand booklet for all employees

Theme days

Company crèche

Six to seven weeks' training for
new representatives

Buddy system and coaching for
new recruits

Incentive payments based on
quality as well as quantity

Call centres measured in terms
of customer satisfaction and
relationships

PLUS benefits package

Communications groups

Direction sessions at the
start of every year

---

doesn't matter, it's the tone of the interaction that matters. If you design an organization which has got its culture and its knowledge systems integrated in a single whole, and you have a mission in life, the interaction between you and your customers is going to be better than that of your competitors.

The organization is designed around the customer, focusing on the single customer at the point of contact. The philosophy makes sense and seems to drive the company forward and is all encompassing. We ensure that our internal brand values are the same as our external ones. It seems to me that there must be a mirror between the two. You can't pretend to be one style of brand to your consumers if you're a different style of brand to your people. It's the people who deliver your company interface, therefore the two have to be the same. We work very, very hard to say the same things to our people as to our customers.

I'm absolutely certain that a successful company employs people who believe in their company and believe in themselves in a way which puts them on the side of the consumer rather than on the side of the organization for which they work. There are three things which you need to do: the first is to make sure that visible signs of organizational structure are taken away if they create barriers to anything which would lead to a good conversation with customers. You won't find any offices in First Direct, you won't find any named car park spaces except for people with disabilities or people bringing kids to the crèche. You won't find any signs of hierarchy. So take away all visible signs of hierarchy. The second thing is to get rid of non-value-creating behaviours. You need to get a culture where things which create barriers are broken down, so you try to work in task forces and cross-functional mode all the time. The third part is to spend some time and effort discussing and implementing behaviours that are going to add value to what you're trying to do.

There's a very low rate of turnover in First Direct compared to competitive call centres. We have communication groups where we take people from different departments into groups of about 10 and they can discuss matters as they wish. We have events where the CEO will talk to all people, twice a year. We have directors available on the floor to talk to people all the time. It's a way of getting conversation between senior management and people on the floor. You've got to believe in this. You must have a belief that all people are equal in terms of the business. First Direct spends a lot of time and effort on this, it's not something which is the province of the personnel function or the motivation unit function or the service function or anything like that, it's the role of all of the organization. It's a deeply philosophical thing, right in the heart of the organization I think.

There is a brand booklet that we produce every four years. By the time we've written it it's out of date because everything is changing. People who join us are given this booklet which defines what the values are and we reinforce those in communications. But I don't think you would get the 4,000 people in First Direct to say the same thing about First Direct in every conversation they have, nor would I want it, to be honest. In the same way we don't have scripting in our telephone conversations, we wouldn't want people to come out with 'First Direct is a leading bank

11

We all dress up like we're having a beach party

in the world' for example, without believing it. We'd rather they put it in their own words and believed what they were saying rather than coming out with something management had told them to say.

Of course, it's absolute folly to think that the people walking through your door are somehow going to change and chant the corporate mantra all the time, it isn't like that. The only difference between work experience and a leisure experience, to me, is that you should be getting paid for the work experience, otherwise they should be equally informative, interesting and part of life's rich pattern. The first thing is, can you make it fun? Secondly, can you make people feel good about themselves? How do you make people feel good about themselves? Well, you have to give them as much personal responsibility, personal authority and control as you possibly can. Whilst you need one or two techniques to measure performance, the real measure of performance is did you have a good day today or didn't you?

We always get the same reaction from first-time visitors to a First Direct building, there's a huge 'buzz' around the place, people are always asking us to define that buzz or for us to come up with some secret ingredient about how it develops. The good news is that there isn't one as far as we can see. It is a combination of factors and basic philosophies of the organization. So it is partly a philosophy thing, do you actually believe it's a good place to work or not. But we use any number of motivational techniques as well. There'll be theme days where we all dress up like we're having a beach party and all that sort of stuff. Now you might think that doesn't make a difference but it does if people are enjoying themselves. Anything you can think of actually to make it more than the average place to work is great.

If you get your customer interfaces right, you're going to get high levels of satisfaction. You need a very high level of satisfaction to generate recommendation between members of the public. First Direct's key is to generate not just satisfied customers but very satisfied customers, they lead to recommendations. Satisfied customers don't. So the good news is that 33 percent of all customers that have joined us have joined us on the basis of personal recommendations. What we're looking for in responding to our customers is that people are smashing, they're wonderful, they're great. Reactions of a more emotional nature which cause the customer to put down the phone and think 'well that was a good experience'. It's those types of reactions which generate differentiation. If you ask our customers, and we do it regularly, to think about us, we get very high scores on the basic objective and rational matters, but we also get very high scores on the more emotional ones. And that's very encouraging because that's where long-term differentiation lies.

Once we reached 1,000 people we feared it would be impossible to get consistency because it would be impossible for senior managers to know everybody and be in touch with the day-to-day environment. However, when we went through that barrier we didn't find a difference which was material, and I think that's because the value set is ingrained in the organization rather than pushed upon it by management. The second hurdle was when we moved to more than one location. We felt the geographical problems would mean that we would be unable to get that same consistency. Incredibly that's just not happened at all. So you go to Glasgow and it's really a fun place, a very exciting place. Now we've moved online, which is the current challenge. It doesn't seem to be affecting us at all, in fact it seems to be adding value. It seems that as long as you don't see one channel eliminating another channel, but see it as an additional form of having good conversations or good interfaces, you are okay. Next year 60 percent of our customers will be banking with us online.

We have this fundamental belief in taking the consumers' point of view first, not a financial services point of view. It's belief in the combination of the integration of knowledge systems and leadership of culture. I think that's the basis of our success. It's not a bad model for anyone in financial services I would say. Happily it's not generally replicated.

David Mead
Chief Operating Officer

First Direct prides itself on consistently delivering long-term value, then underpinning that long-term value with a personalized banking service based around the organization knowing each individual customer. In terms of the delivery of that differentiated service proposition, there are a number of critical things that contribute. First of all, from an organizational design point of view, we are very customer-centric and so we have shied away from, and positively reject, if you will, the traditional product line design of the organization. Instead we have built an organizational design that has all of the people who face the customer working together. What we end up with is a situation where we give prominence to customer needs rather than specific products. The second key enabler would be the harnessing of information. We track customer behaviour, including channels used, frequency of telephone calls, the nature of the transactions effected over those different channels, with a view to anticipating the next action on behalf of the customer so that we can 'sell to need'. That puts First Direct proactively on the side of the customer.

Of primary importance, among our people, is personality and empathy and genuine passion for customer service. Secondary importance is systems understanding and product knowledge, both of which can be trained. The former, ie, the personality and passion for customer service can't, they tend to be more innate traits, so the concentration of recruitment is to get the right people and then equip them with the right knowledge and confidence, and they will then deliver the superior and differentiated service that we talk about.

The training of the representatives is extremely thorough. We continue to invest about six or seven weeks in representatives when they first join us before they are in dialogue with customers. At the point where they come out of training, they buddy up with colleagues. They have coaches and they have a team leader who invests, initially, a disproportionate amount of time in coaching and

11

Our call centres are measured in terms of customer satisfaction and broadening and deepening the relationship the customer has with us

support activities, so they are monitoring and identifying opportunities to improve the customer dialogue and the customer experience. We have very clear contribution statements for our people that not only focus on sales or productivity, they also focus crucially on the quality of the dialogue that they're having with the customer and that drives individuals' incentive payments at the end of the year. So the reward strategy is very much focused on ensuring people continue to place emphasis on quality as well as on quantity.

We obviously do extensive customer research and that research goes on through the life cycle of the customer's relationship with us, starting with feedback after only 90 days of a new customer joining us and then, thereafter, periodically in order to make sure that from a customer satisfaction point of view we're continuing to maintain our standards. What is very clear is that the way in which we live the core values means that we effectively empower people to engage in dialogue, truly understand the customer need and then deliver against that need. In many respects the customer research that is done still shows that our customers feel that they get more personalized service from our direct banking proposition than they do from face-to-face banking in many cases. Sustaining that can only come ultimately from placing trust in our customer representatives, who exercise their judgement at the point of customer interaction in terms of 'wowing' the customer. What we've tended to reject consistently is embracing a lot of rules and regulations that would potentially constrain our representatives from, let's say, spending enough time on the telephone. A lot of call centres are judged on call duration and maximising productivity. Our call centres are measured in terms of customer satisfaction and broadening and deepening the relationship the customer has with us.

We have a direction session at the start of every year at which we say, 'these are the key challenges of the business and this is how we intend to approach them, now let's get everyone engaged and focused on delivering their individual part of that'. So there is a variety of mechanisms for engaging people, getting people to internalize business strategy and core values. Some of the things we do are slightly off the wall, but we consistently argue that one of the underlying principles that we seek to adhere to is that of individuality. We passionately believe that every customer is an individual and requires a unique and personalized service. To make sure that our people genuinely believe that and believe that principle on each and every occasion, we also focus very strongly on the individual within First Direct. For example, rather than having a standard set of benefits that people can utilize in terms of their reward package, we have a package called PLUS which effectively enables the individual to tailor their particular benefits to their stage in their life. In order to reinforce the primary importance of individuality with the customer, we seek to do the same with our people, so we talk about individual people here in the same way as we talk about individual customers externally.

Any leader within the organization who pays lip service to the core values would stand out 'like a sore thumb' and would either get some very active coaching to get aligned or may take a decision that this place wasn't right for them. It means, on occasion, that the culture is intolerant of other ways of running a business but if you believe you have a winning culture you tend to want to reinforce that. The final piece, for me, is around a real passion for customers and an insistence that in every decision made, the leader has a clear line of sight about what the customer experience will be as a result of the initiative that they're advocating or endorsing.

Ewan Hutton
Head of Electronic Services

We see a single customer/bank relationship. As a customer you may elect to bank with us using only one channel, so you may decide you only want to use the telephone, and that's cool. Or you may decide that you want to use internet banking too: you may use our website as well, you may also use our mobile services, that doesn't change how we view you as a customer. All of those different channels are fully integrated at the bank, so that means if you happen to be using one channel to do something and you're having a conversation with an agent on the telephone, or you're online or whatever, whether you're paying a bill, requesting a product, or whether we're trying to sell you something, each of the channels knows what has happened on the other channel simultaneously. So if you've having a conversation with one of our agents about a loan and we were about to post a brochure to see if you're interested in loans that would be stopped that day, unless it's already gone in the post. The same with online teasers, if you've logged in and there's a banner telling you that you can have a given loan amount, that would stop instantly if you had already spoken to the call centre about it, and vice versa. It's a holistic approach. One customer and one set of information.

That ethos or approach applies to everything we do. It applies to how we design new systems and new products and it applies to how we run our departments. Yes, we have separate functions and manage the customer's experience from them but it's part of the total experience. Customer-relationship management has been at the heart of our organization from the start. This is critical now given the mix of contact channels, and that 50 percent of our business is now electronic.

We have politics, we have all that stuff, we're humans, I'm afraid that happens but not over the customers, that's the holy grail. For example, if a call comes into a call centre and a customer has a complaint about something, the agent who takes the call will take that complaint and own it right through the organization, that means going to the CEO and saying we need a signed response from you on it. It may seem overblown, but it demonstrates the customer-centric culture.

HOTELS & RESORTS

12

The Fairmont brand has stood for luxury accommodation since its very inception in 1884. Over the years it has continually won plaudits for its uncompromising approach to guest satisfaction. Yet this is not one of the 'grand old ladies' of the industry continuing to trade on past reputation. The organization has grown rapidly by amalgamating three individual brands to create a proposition which sets out to offer guests memorable resort experiences.

The focus on hiring the best people, training and leadership development has created high morale and satisfied employees. Not surprisingly, Fairmont has been cited as one of the 35 best employers to work for in Canada. This clear strategy, strong alignment between functions and a culture of quality and service in everything they do has enabled the brand to successfully dominate the Condé Nast Traveler's Readers' Choice Poll with no less than half of its 38 hotels and resorts appearing in the magazine's coveted 2001 Gold List.

Bill Fatt

Chief Executive Officer

To understand the Fairmont brand, you have to understand that we really are an amalgamation of three brands that were put together in late 1999. We had the Canadian Pacific brand, which was very strong in Canada. We had the Princess brand, which consisted of seven resort properties that Canadian Pacific Hotels acquired in August of '98 and then the Fairmont brand, which, at the time of acquisition included seven US city-centre properties. All of our luxury properties are now reflagged under the Fairmont brand throughout North America. When we put the companies together, each of them obviously had different practices and procedures and what we've tried to do is to take a collection of the best practices in order to ensure that we have the proper service delivery. And, we focus very much on employees in terms of service delivery. The three basic factors that will ensure success for a hotel company are location, product and service. And because we're an old company with heritage assets, we tend to have very good locations.

We've spent a lot of money on the product so we're quite proud of our assets. But service delivery is really the key. The people working within the hotels are the ones who have the face-to-face contact with the customers and they are the most important part of the overall equation of meeting the promise that the brand represents. We try to select the best and then we train them. We have to make sure that they are properly motivated and then recognized as they deliver service.

The Fairmont brand is a luxury brand, so it stands for absolutely first class accommodation. We tend to be concentrated in larger assets, although we do have two or three quite small, almost boutique, hotels. In addition, we have more heritage properties than many competitors. A little more than half of our hotels are resort hotels, which is unusual. And particularly in resorts you want to try to provide a total experience for your guests, as opposed to simply a building and a room to rest in. Our resort assets have spectacular locations and we have a full range of services – like spas, golf courses, ski facilities – not necessarily that we own but adjacent to our resort properties.

We have a team that is focused on making sure that our employees are properly positioned to be able to provide these guest experiences. The service culture and the focus on making sure that the guest has a positive experience runs throughout the team. Everything that we do has to be measured against whether or not it's going to enhance the guest experience.

Marketing has to make sure that what we are saying about our properties and our services is consistent with our ability to deliver. This is so that when guests read about our promises and then arrive at our properties, they know what to expect and they're fully satisfied with what we are able to offer them. The Fairmont brand represents over 80 percent of the company and that's where we believe we have the best ability to grow. Enhancing the brand, increasing consumer awareness and furthering the guest loyalty that we've been able to create is a huge part of our corporate strategy.

'Uncommon Practice' at Fairmont Hotels

Service level measured constantly

Service Plus HR strategy

My Fairmont Service Plus orientation training programme

Service Plus recognition programme

Annual employee-satisfaction surveys

Focus groups and surveys

Presidents' Club recognition programme

Building the brand is absolutely critical and was a central part of why we acquired Fairmont. We wanted to grow outside of Canada, but our belief was that the Canadian Pacific brand would not travel well outside of the country. So, having a brand name that represented an image in consumers' minds, that was comparable or compatible with our properties, and that had a reasonable degree of recognition in the very large US marketplace, was critical to our strategy.

I spend an awful lot of my time on things like growth, investor relations and generally setting the strategy for the overall company. When you look at growth, you have to have a strong brand in order to convince yourself that you can add value to properties that you're either going to acquire or manage for others. So building and enhancing the reputation of the Fairmont brand is critical from the growth perspective. In order to build and sustain the brand, you have to make sure that the product meets today's needs. One of the things that has happened over the last few years is the increasing need for technology both to be able to serve guests, and to be available for guests to use when they're visiting our properties. So, a very important function for us is keeping up with the changing needs of consumers, particularly in the technology area – whether it's restaurants or food services that we provide, or the types of property experiences that guests want, or any one of a number of things. The levels of service that employees are expected to provide constantly have to be measured against changing customer demands and the competitive marketplace. We constantly have to survey our customers and make sure that we understand what services are required and we adapt accordingly.

We've invested heavily in information technology to create databases of guest profiles and we are able to understand what services guests are using. We have significant communication with our guests in order to better understand their service needs. And, obviously, we watch trends in the industry. So it's a combination of those things that gives us the confidence to make these large commitments.

You have to do a tremendous amount of research to understand your customer profile. We spent a lot of money on focus groups and surveys. Before we did a huge amount in this area, we tried to come up with a pretty fixed view as to the niche that we would be able to operate in and provide a unique service to. So doing your research in advance is hugely important.

When I think back over the last three years, on reflection, I would have tried to introduce these changes more quickly than, in fact, happened. But the difficulty in a large organization like ours is that you have to make changes at a pace that the organization can handle. We are still rolling out additional guest services all of the time and these things just take time to perfect. It's really a question of prioritizing. We can come up with hundreds of ideas on things that would be nice to have but we recognize that these are expensive and take time, training and effort to put in place and execute. So we've tried to focus on what we believe are a priority. Guest service is priority number one so there is nothing that takes us away from trying to provide guests with the absolute best service possible.

12

Chris Cahill

President and Chief Operating Officer

I believe that employees interpret the brand based on everything from the imaging, the words we use and how we've adjusted the mission statement, vision and values

I think if I were to define our service culture, it would be it's a caring, professional, respectful service orientation. This is not inconsistent with our positioning as a brand. I think the underlying promise is probably dependability. It's a funny word but I think our brand should be rock solid in the minds of the consumers. They should have an expectation that they will not be disappointed. Because of the uniqueness of our product, it's not going to be a 'cookie cutter' and so we're focused on the customization of individual guest experiences. For example, I want people who are in our Presidents' Club, which is our recognition programme, to get the same experience when they arrive at our hotel that I get. I want to feel that the hotel knows I'm coming, that they know who I am, and my room is what I want it to be. And whether it's the CDs, jazz instead of classical, or whether it's magazines, I want the room to reflect my pattern of stay and experience. So that's what we're putting in place to try to accelerate our brand-building exercise. Behind that is the whole human resource process.

I believe that employees interpret the brand based on everything from the imaging and the new human resource language, the words we use and how we've adjusted the mission statement, vision and values. They're 'getting it', and it's permeating throughout the company. But I think, as with any organization that's been around a long time, you get people's view of what the brand means as opposed to what it actually does mean. So one of the things we've also done is to align our performance management process and goals and targets with the brand to drive the behaviour that we expect out of the brand.

We have three strategic priorities. One is to energize the brand and that comes from a combination of operating the branding, the consistency and the focus. The second priority is to maximize the performance of the assets. That's a matter of capital enhancements and we've got tremendous opportunities in this regard. A third priority is to mobilize the company around growth. So we've taken those three priorities and we've taken the four constituents we work with – the employee, the customer, the owner/shareholder and the brand – and we've created a matrix. We've established measurements in each of the quadrants of the matrix to indicate what we measure against and what constitutes success. And then we've established hard targets to measure success in each box. So, for example, under energizing the brand as it relates to the customer, would be market share. So everybody's clear on what's important and the measures that are within their line of sight. Everything comes back to the brand. I think there are three things that I have learned: one, you need to be very clear on what the brand or the product represents to your customers, how they think about it. You have to be really clear and really honest about that. Two, you have to have a compelling internal vision that your employees on all levels can relate to. And three, I think you've got to get the strategy to a point where what you're trying to accomplish can be clearly articulated. Then you have to communicate like hell.

Carolyn Clark

Vice-President, Human Resources

Our company's mission is to 'earn the loyalty of our guests by exceeding their expectations and providing warm and personal service in distinctive surroundings'. The key words for us are 'earning the loyalty of our guests' and 'exceeding expectations'. We want to deliver service value and provide an experience that is far beyond what any one of our guests would have ever imagined.

What we have achieved did not happen by chance. We began our journey in 1988 when we launched a programme to restore all of our hotels. We were investing $750 million of capital and realized that if we didn't put as much emphasis on the service delivery and human development part of our business, we wouldn't be able to provide the necessary rate of return to our shareholders or owners. So, it was at that point we developed an integrated human resource strategy, which we call 'Service Plus', our internal human resource brand. It has four key components – select, lead, train and reward. Each of these components must be an integral part of our human resource culture in order for us to achieve our mission. Every person who is hired in the company, from our room attendants to our executive vice-president, goes through a structured interview which helps us identify individuals who have a natural service orientation. Based on the information we gain, we are able to put people into jobs where they can do lots of what they're naturally good at, as opposed to putting someone who has no service orientation into a front-office position. People who have a natural service orientation inherently want to provide great service to our guests in order to exceed their expectations. These people are passionate about service delivery.

Once we hire all these great people, we know that great people need great leaders. So we developed a structured interview to help us select great leaders. We've learned through our research that people don't quit their companies, they quit their leaders, so you've got to have strong leadership in place in order to move the service culture forward. Great people who are working with great leaders also need training. They need to grow and develop personally so we designed and implemented a service training programme. Finally, our colleagues need to be recognized for their service efforts so we put into place the fourth component, which is our Service Plus Recognition Programme.

With our recent re-branding and our HR strategy, we're really, really excited. I think this will position us in terms of delivering the brand experience. We know that marketing and sales will bring our guests to the brand the first time but it's the service experience they receive that will keep them coming back. And it is every one of our employees who must deliver the brand promise. We have developed a new colleague orientation programme which we call 'My Fairmont Service Plus'. It's more than an orientation; it's also our service training programme. The goal of every single colleague is to provide WOW experiences that will create memories for all guests of Fairmont Hotels & Resorts. If every single one of our 22,000 colleagues comes to work every day with a

People don't quit their companies, they quit their leaders

personal mission statement that says 'My goal is to provide WOW experiences for my guests, then I am delivering on the brand promise' that's all they need to remember.

To ensure we are on track and all of our hotels' human resource practices are aligned, we conduct annual employee-satisfaction surveys. These surveys produce a percentile score and it is our goal as a company to be a top quartile employer in terms of positioning ourselves as an employer of choice. Each one of our hotels has a target score (out of 100). Under that, each department also has a target score that is translated into our management incentive plan. Keeping our eye on these targets is critically important to us, as our research indicates there is a direct correlation between our employee satisfaction and guest satisfaction; the hotels with the highest employee satisfaction also have the highest guest satisfaction scores.

Service delivery is at the core of our brand experience. And it's our front-line colleagues who provide that service delivery. It's not the general managers sitting in their office. It's not the executive committee member who has that contact with the guest. These individuals must be given the training and the tools to provide support to the real service providers – our front-line colleagues.

At our last general managers' conference, Brian Richardson, Vice-President, Marketing, stressed that we all carry the title 'Brand Manager' on our business cards and that brand management is not confined to the role of corporate marketing. Every time we are meeting with a guest, every time we go out and make sales calls, and every day when we provide service in our hotels, we are Fairmont brand managers. It means knowing what differentiates Fairmont Hotels & Resorts from our competitors. It means translating our brand into the personal behaviours of each of our 22,000 colleagues every day.

Brian Richardson

Vice-President, Marketing

Knowing we were going to adopt the Fairmont brand and migrate away from Canadian Pacific as our brand, we took a step back last year. We really tried to start from a brand perspective which touches on the customer experience. We went through a very rigorous and robust process over the course of six months; we tried to address two things: who our primary target audience is and should be, and what our brand positioning should be. An equation started to build in all these conversations. One that was most favourably received was the notion of 'fabric of community' and 'prominence'. The consumers said these two elements are the essence of the 'Fairmont' brand, and that we could translate these into an enriched stay for the customer. If creating memories is important to you, we believe we have the ability to do that. If staying at the right address is important to you, we believe we can deliver on that. Because of what we are, because we comprise the types of hotels that we have, because they are what they are in the community in which they reside, we think that represents a better stay, an enriched stay.

I think brand positioning is bigger than customer communications. We've had a lot of discussion about how it should affect the way the employees think about the brand. We (marketing) started it and then worked with HR to refine it. I think it would be incredibly powerful if every employee came to work every day thinking about the brand and his or her role in delivering it.

We want employees to think about their role in enriching the experience of the guests in our hotel who are visitors to our city. That means doing little things that don't cost anything but mean so much. We want our colleagues to think about this notion of fabric of community and we want them to go beyond thinking about the experience as starting and ending at our door. So the positioning statement, communications and the employee covenant are all tied into the brand. It needs to affect communications, it needs to affect employee behaviour, it needs to literally affect what we do on site from an operational perspective.

RBC Financial Group

13

Banks are not usually noted for their concern for others, yet RBC Financial Group has been voted Canada's top company in the area of corporate responsibility for six years in a row. For the past three years it has been named as Canada's most respected corporation for people management. And yes, it gets the numbers right too, being ranked highest of all Canadian companies for financial performance. Not content with that, the brand has attracted accolades for its telephone banking, online banking and customer relationship manager systems. Perhaps this is why 40 percent of all adult Canadians bank with RBC.

What is also uncommon in an organization so successful in its marketplace is the unrelenting focus on improving performance. The absolute focus on customer needs, and the systems and processes that are geared towards equipping people with the knowledge, tools and rewards to meet them profitably, has created a brand that is held in high esteem by all its stakeholders.

Jim Rager

Vice-Chair, Personal & Commercial Banking

First, you must have knowledge of your clients and be willing to make resource allocation decisions or investments to enhance the capability that you need. You have to invest day-to-day. You need to invest in customer analytics. We prioritize those decisions at the most senior levels of our business.

Second, you need to be organized in a way that allows you to deliver. We have moved away from a traditional, retail business, menu approach, into one that is driven by segment managers. We have been relentless by having everything aligned with what those segment managers say we need to do. I live and breathe that. It has to be my belief and my point of view about this industry and what it takes to succeed.

You need alignment to deliver the strategy. You have to be a believer in it and talk about it in the right way with people in all parts of the organization. You have to spend a lot of time. You have to be engaged in it. You have to be out there in it. You cannot just sit back and view it as somebody else's job.

With the type of organization we used to be, it was very difficult to be integrated properly and to have the right actions and execution strategies in place to deliver an integrated, consistent approach. We had somebody over there running business banking with all of their data and strategies and channel plans, and another person over here running credit cards, and another person over here running retail banking, each with business goals related to those products' lines or customer segments. We could not get enough common approach with that type of organization, so we eliminated that structure about two years ago. When we did, some people left, including senior people. Others didn't leave but were moved around. We reorganized in the way that we now have it. I would say at least half of the senior leadership group changed. The change was designed to deliver the brand strategy – that brand promise. It was hard because we had run things on a product basis. All of our decisions, all of our resource allocations, all of the bottom line accountability used to be driven by the products.

The different parts of our traditional businesses – the silos like business banking, retail banking and credit cards – had different capabilities in terms of data and how they used it. It was hard to get everybody, all of a sudden, up to speed at the same level at the same time. That was difficult. A cultural change results from the fact that you're valuing one set of capabilities *vis-à-vis* others. For instance, suddenly you are reinforcing behaviours now with a broader customer perspective versus a narrower product or channel view.

What we learned was that you have to be ready, meaning you must have core capabilities that you have developed, mostly with your data and your segmentation of that data, before you can jump into this. The other thing is to do it fast. We decided to say in February this is the new organization

'Uncommon Practice' at RBC Financial Group

Sales management wheel

'I make it right' problem resolution programme

Total rewards programme for employees

Performance management and coaching programme

and how we are going to approach the business. We said that by November 1 we would be all done and ready to go and take risks along the way. You just have to do it or not.

If the strategy of your business is to deliver the brand, you have to have people developing the execution side of all that. Then through your delivery channels, make sure that everybody is aligned. The thing that we are happiest and proudest about is that we have managed our alignment. If you go to Saskatchewan or Alberta or Newfoundland, you will hear people talking about this in the same way: in the same theme, same activities, same understanding of what they have to do and what this is all about. People bring it to life.

If your brand promise is to understand customers, anticipate their needs and give advice, you have to convert the mindset in your traditional branches from selling a credit product or a deposit product to wanting to understand the customer's need. This means a lot of training; an evolution, changing people and sales management out there to get you through. In order to do that, you need to have the technology and the processes in place. In an organization as large as ours with 1,300 branches and 30,000 people, to achieve that consistently and quickly, you have to have the processes as well as the right technology.

The biggest differentiator that we have is what we call our 'sales management wheel'. This is a continuum of things related to training, professional designations, technology, rewards and recognition. All of those things have to be pulled together to make change work. Whenever we want to change something, whether it be goals, an approach, or going into a different market segment that we had ignored, we immediately create a total alignment of all of those things. When we spit it out at the other end in terms of what people have to do, the rewards are aligned with what it is we are asking of people. If we need to train them, we do it. If the technology or the sales platform needs to be modified in some way to support that, we do it. You have to think about change in a very integrated and aligned way. Otherwise you get the wrong behaviours.

My major activity is monthly sales calls that I started about two to three years ago. It does a couple of things: it reinforces the message, it forces discussion. We went through a change from a culture of general managers who cared about the balance sheet, the income statement and how much real estate we had, to one of we don't really care any more about your balance sheet or your income statement, we care about your sales activities. You have to push it in a different way. Also, it's a good way to stay connected to what's going on. I want to hear what is really happening with the mortgage pipelines and with this and that. It relates to leadership overall and to the cultural change we're trying to accomplish, as well as a better way, in my view, to stay up with what's happening in the business.

Going back, say, to the '95/'96 timeframe, the conventional wisdom in this business was that the banks were dinosaurs and wealth management companies were going to take over the world. The only thing that you could do, if you were a traditional banker, was to fold up your network, close it

109

down, cut your costs, become a monoline player in some way, or you were going to lose. We just didn't believe that. We thought that we still had a lot of potential to grow and that the best way of doing that was through a better integration of all of the things that we had. Why do we have to think about retention and growth as being the driver of everything we do? It's because we have 10 million clients. Forty percent of adult Canadians deal with us, but we don't have all of their business. Going after our existing, interesting client base is the easiest way to grow in a market that's relatively small and where everything is bought up already. To do that, you have to think in terms of integration, you have to think in terms of group referrals, multiple channels and consistency across channels. It's been by design, but as we have gone forward, we have become more and more relentless about it.

What I am most proud of right now is that we are achieving the performance levels that we set in all of our measures. Earnings growth is 25 percent. Return of earnings is getting close to 25 percent. Revenue growth is 8 to 10 percent right now, which is hard to come by. We've improved efficiency. The whole strategy as it relates to performance is working.

Judith Hatley

Vice-President, Marketing & Customer Management

Customer-relationship management has become our business model. It's not a project, it's the way we do things around here. In 1992, we launched a project that sorted our customers. We coded them A, B and C and figured out on a monthly basis the net income after tax for every customer. Our objective was to retain and grow the A-coded customers; really get our arms around them. People in our branches didn't know their A-coded customers. They were so focused on being loan officers and the big surprise was that many of the A-coded customers were investment clients. They knew their job was to know their customers – but they didn't know the top 100 of their customers. After that we implemented many initiatives to get in touch with those customers, linking them up with a banker and really trying to differentiate the service.

In the old days we would have product campaigns and maybe talk to a client about a product that they already had. Now, we are able to identify needs and goals for specific customers whether it is through face-to-face contact or direct mail. We are building something called customer preference and choice. We are building capability so that we keep out personal information about how individuals want to be served. For example, 'don't ever call me up after seven o'clock in the evening', or, 'please call me at work'.

To really deliver on the brand promise, we've got to be able to capture the hearts and the minds of people. We focus on four things: greeting customers warmly, calling them by name every time, thanking them for the business and asking them if there is anything we can do to help them. And we measure that; currently we're up over the 90 percent level.

To really deliver on the brand promise, we've got to be able to capture the hearts and the minds of people

We introduced a number of years ago 'I make it right', a problem resolution programme. We took a look at how we handled people problems. We would look at the problem, find out what happened and then explain what happened. But the customers didn't care about why it happened. We had quite a behaviour change to make there. We created 'I make it right', a four-step process. We gave the authority to every person who touched a customer to 'do something to make it right, giving them discretion up to $1,000. It was a big decision. I felt comfortable with it though because I know what okay bankers are. The bigger challenge we had was getting them to use the money. I remember talking to one of the vice-chairmen after we launched the programme. He said, 'What happens to the banker when they run out of the $1,000?' I said, 'No. This is $1,000 per transaction!' Multiply that by 30,000 bankers! In another culture this might not have worked.

Anne Lockie

Executive Vice-President, Marketing & Sales

We turned the organization around and put in place customer segment managers. These individuals drive the strategy for a group of customers and have accountability to the organization for the profitability of those customers. They are the catalysts and bring together all the resources of the organization, including the product people, the marketing team and anybody else they need. They help us to decide what things we need, both for the short and long term, to improve that lifetime value of the client.

We want to be a customer-driven organization. We want to build relationships as a core of what we do. This is a relationship strategy, clear and simple. It is about making every one of our customers profitable. People talk about customers you can't afford to do business with – well, there may be some of them still but there can't be as many as we had. We thought that there was an opportunity to do things differently. We are doing two things at once: generating more revenue by selling more products to the right customers and also streamlining some of the things we do. We talk about the tailored customer experience. It results from what we know about our customer, what we do with that information, and how we implement it at the front line.

We have engineered a sales process with well-defined components. We have a sales process that everyone in the organization follows – from me to every individual salesperson. We all do the same goal setting and reviews. I do it with the heads of our geographies monthly. Many of them do it with their people every two weeks. Once it gets to the direct sales manager levels, we have weekly goals but it's all the same process.

We build very defined roles, very defined accountabilities to facilitate proactive contact and financial advice. We send leads that we generate straight to the desktops of our salespeople. So every day salespeople have a 'to-do' list. What we don't want them to do is spend time wondering – 'What customer should I contact and talk to today and what should I talk to them about?' Every person would come up with a different idea of what they should do, and when. By generating leading we get consistency and most important is that whether or not the client is sitting down with someone in a branch, or whether they call into the call centre at midnight, they will get the same discussion about the same offer and the same opportunity in the same way.

Elisabetta Bigsby

Executive Vice-President, Human Resources & Public Affairs

The brand promise for the personal and commercial bank is about helping the customer achieve whatever they want to achieve; this is in contrast with telling the customer what to do. There are a number of things that we do to support the employee in delivering that promise. We have made quite a bit of progress with the concept of 'total rewards' which includes learning and development, work, life, balance, compensation and benefits, and career opportunities. 'Total rewards' is the result of various components that work in different ways at different times for people. The core issue is to portray our corporation to the employee as one that is interested in their development, is respectful of their situation, is ready to reward them appropriately if they perform, and give them opportunities to advance. All of those things are related to the brand promise.

We know that the corporate positioning has about three times more impact on employee behaviours than their unit positioning. As a result, we are focused on corporate strategy, corporate values, corporate communications, corporate total rewards, corporate programmes for work/life balance; because that is what helps people in the units. We cannot afford to have a situation where the corporation and the unit are speaking different languages; the employee will hear the corporation, not the unit.

We construct the HR strategic plan at the corporate and at the various business platform levels. Both of these are a result of reviewing the business strategic plan and asking what HR can do to facilitate the progress of the business towards achieving its strategic goals; HR is now part of the leadership group. We believe very strongly that compensation is not the right tool to manage change effectively. Performance management is the right tool to establish personal goals aligned with strategy, supported by coaching clearly measured and adequately rewarded.

You need to put in place the leadership and communication that enables people to deliver what it is that they should deliver. If they cannot deliver, it will fail and will be a gigantic source of frustration to them personally. The key is to never over promise and, by and large, to ensure that whatever you have promised is actually deliverable. With this approach the employee experience becomes a source of satisfaction in being able to do a good job rather than a source of aggravation because of promises that cannot be kept. Another way of putting it is that people are much more engaged if they're having fun than if they aren't. So if we put them in a place where they can actually succeed, it will work.

Our approach goes like this: these are the values, values generate leadership behaviours, leadership behaviours generate management practices, management practices touch six or seven things that affect employee commitment and employee commitment affects customer satisfaction. That's how we go about it. Values and the brand promise intermingle in different ways but it is easier to connect with the employee from the values point of view. Naturally the expression of the values and the brand promise need to be consistent but in the end one gets to the same place.

Jennifer Tory
Senior Vice-President, Sales Effectiveness

Every customer experience is the responsibility of somebody, whether it's the person at the front line or the person in a support environment. If the messages they are getting about how to deliver the customer experience in the best way are not consistent then, obviously, they're not going to be clear about what they're supposed to do. That's why leadership reinforcement of our expectations around the customer experience is so critical. The way we have aligned ourselves in terms of leadership measurement and reward and recognition, both in the field and in the centres, all the way up to the chairman, is so that everyone understands that their responsibility is to deliver the customer experience. The question is do they always feel they have the resources or the tools to do that? We're continually reinforcing with the leaders that they have to let us know when they don't have the tools. Alignment, in terms of understanding what our strategy is around the customer experience, is critical.

THE Carphone Warehouse
COMMUNICATION CENTRES

14

Founded in 1989 by a handful of people with minimal capital, Carphone Warehouse now has more than 5,500 staff in over 1,050 stores in 12 countries; turnover for the year ending March 2001 was £1.1 billion.

From its outset, it has offered exceptional customer value while refusing to tie itself to any one phone network, a principle summarized in its brand promise of 'simple – impartial – advice'. Its dedication to exceeding customers' expectations has been rewarded consistently over the years with a clutch of awards for customer service, its people and the culture it has created.

Compared to any other retailer, Carphone Warehouse invests four times the average on training; sales executives, regarded as the company heroes, have to undertake an intensive, two-week training course before greeting their first customer. The open management style, flat structure and belief that 'the reputation of the entire company is in the hands of every individual' has been central to its success in a dynamic and rapidly moving industry.

THE Carphone Warehouse

COMMUNICATION CENTRE

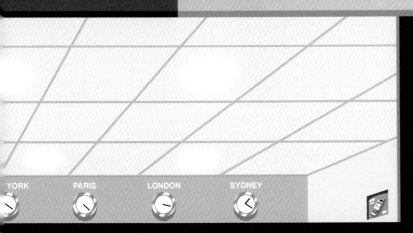

YORK   PARIS   LONDON   SYDNEY

fascias

ALL THE TARIFFS   ALL THE NETWORKS   ALL THE TARIFFS

FREE UPGRADE   MOBILE PHONES   FOOTBALL SCORES DIRECT TO YOUR PHONE

Goal Flash

your mobile

Charles Dunstone

Chief Executive Officer

When we first started the business what we do didn't exist. If you wanted to buy a phone and you were in a large organization which had a purchasing department, you bought them directly from the networks but if not you had to go to a car stereo shop or somewhere under the arches. So we said 'why shouldn't people who work for smaller businesses, or private individuals, have the same opportunity to buy a phone and have it properly looked after like a large corporation?' We started with £6,000, less than half a dozen people, no experience in retail, no heritage, nothing. If you're not absolutely set in your mind that you're going to do a better job than anyone else, to look after customers and to earn their money, and if you don't really understand how you're going to add value to customers, then you're not going to succeed. If you have no money and no brand you'll never succeed. It's astonishing really that we've managed to get away with it.

One of the things that makes this organization different is that people at all levels of the company are much closer to customers than they would be elsewhere and much more focused. We debate the smallest intricacies of our proposition to customers and how we deliver it. I like debating it as a company. For example in the UK we fix a lot of phones for customers, about 10,000 a week, about half of which we didn't supply in the first place and all our competitors send their customers to us, which we love. But it actually costs us an enormous amount to do it. So, we're debating whether we should say 'we're delighted to fix it for you, it will be no problem at all, this is how we'll fix it, but there's a £10 handling charge which is refunded if you ever buy anything at Carphone Warehouse'. That's an idea that someone came up with in one part of the business, it then got socialized in the business here and I sent an email to all the store managers saying 'got this idea, what do you think? How do you think people are going to react?' Very mixed response, some people saying 'no, it's central to what we do, we're always there for customers wherever they've bought their phone, it's very un-Carphone Warehouse to do this'. Others saying 'no, that's fair because why should you get all the benefits of being in the club if you've not joined the club' and we're saying 'you can join the club anyway because you get the money back'. So we take soundings and refine the idea. People are very involved in the process of decision making and there aren't any really big secrets.

Our finance teams sigh at times with the things that we do because we do things that frighten them. The greatest example is 'the ultimate price promise', which is the best single thing we've ever done: if you buy a phone from us, 90 days after you've bought it, our computer compares the price you've paid with the price we now sell it for. If it's fallen in price we automatically mail you a voucher for the difference without you ever having to ask. Now you can imagine a finance team being absolutely horrified. It's not insubstantial sums of money. In the last 14 months we've given away £10 million to customers, but they are astounded when they get it; they can't believe that

'Uncommon Practice' at Carphone Warehouse

Two-week residential training course for all recruits

Conventions for store managers

Employee-attitude survey

Monthly beer bus

Annual ball

Company rules on business cards

Company performance sent to employees by text message

Promote internally wherever possible

Invest four times the average amount on training compared to other retailers

Ongoing training on intranet

Ongoing training workshops

'Maximise' people performance scheme

Employees encouraged to email directly to CEO

any company would do that. When you start to do the ultimate price promise you can do a little spreadsheet and make some assumptions, but until you do it you don't know what the redemption rate is going to be, what they are going to buy with it. Eventually the guy from the accounts team said 'alright where are we going to test it?', the response to which was 'no, we can't test it, that's so unfair, if you bought your phone in Liverpool you got the refund but if you bought your phone in Leeds you didn't'. We have to do it everywhere, and if it doesn't work in three months' time we have to stop it, but if we do it, we do it. We've proven over time that these initiatives do work. We have this idea, I don't know where I picked it up from, 'visionary ideas turn strangers into customers' and if you do things that are really different, that are beyond what people expect, then you do turn strangers into customers. Then if you do a great job, you can turn your customers into advocates.

I don't think I was terribly confident in my heart to begin with. I felt we should do things this way, but I had a suspicion, as most people do, that if you do these things you don't make any money. So what's been a great revelation to me is that the more we do these things, the more successful we've been. I think you can treat the people that work for you with dignity and respect, I think you can do a great job for customers and be very successful – there are many people who would imagine that softness would actually have a bad effect on their financial results.

We're organized like any normal company. We've got a sales team, an HR team, an accounts team and a marketing team, but what is unique, I think, is that within our business everybody absolutely understands what we stand for and what's expected of them. I never talk to anyone in the stores about their sales figures. I only ever talk to them about what customers are saying and customer service. We talk about things as being a 'Carphone Warehouse thing to do' or 'not a Carphone Warehouse thing to do', we talk about people we might recruit as being a Carphone Warehouse person or not being a Carphone Warehouse person.

We manage our employee retention in two ways; we'll manage our turnover in general but, specifically, what we really focus on is the number of people that leave us to go and work for the competition. If you worked for us and decided you wanted to become a teacher or something that's absolutely fine, you make a vocational change I've got no issues with that at all, if you leave us to go and work for a competitor, then we've failed.

Our training development starts with a two-week residential course that you have to attend before being allowed to work in the stores. We spend an enormous amount of money on training – if you walk into one of our shops you expect the people to know what they're talking about. We don't do 'close the sale' training, we do 'how Vodafone works' training. So we're not looking for salespeople, we just want nice people who are reasonably good communicators.

We have big conventions for all our store managers with tons of feedback, appraisals and suggestion schemes; we have an attitude survey we've done with everybody, there's a lot of dialogue. One of the things that's still very important to me is that anybody can feel that they can send me an email

– and they do! They might be 'why don't we open shops in Pakistan?' to 'how come when I sell this customers seem to want that and we don't seem to offer it?'

We have an expression that says 'do we run our company for the 97 percent of our customers who are honest or do we run it to protect ourselves from the 3 percent that aren't?' The bigger you get, the more the organization focuses on the 3 percent because the more system-driven it becomes. And the more remote the people that are taking the calls from customers become. I try and circumvent that by really being close to the people in the stores and I try to be their champion. We get out to the stores a lot. People really need a figurehead and they need something to believe in.

We never call people here staff because we think staff is somehow a bit patronizing to people and none of our businesses is allowed to have a head office, we call this place a support centre. They're simple things but they're important. Some people think we're nuts but I think it's really important to keep pushing that, it sends a big message to people. We have this beer bus once a month for everyone in the company, we throw a big ball once a year. But a lot of it really is just the pride and the sort of mutual responsibility that you have. We have five fundamental rules that everyone has to learn, and they're on our business cards and the last rule of them all is 'the reputation of the entire company is in the hands of every individual'. And we drum into people very hard that every single time they talk to customers, they've actually got every single one of us sat on their shoulders, we're dependent on every word that they say and their customers are going to judge us entirely by that. I think the most important thing to say, also, is we're far from perfect, we get stuff wrong a lot of the time. Not only do we get stuff wrong, sometimes we'll then compound the error in a way that when you finally get to look at it you think 'how can we have contrived to do all of this to this one poor person?' But every time we do something wrong, you can actually go back to one of those rules and where it's gone wrong is in not following one of those rules.

Our sales figures are shown within the company, as much information as we can legally make available is available to people. So if you work in our logistics team and you haven't got the right stock in the right stores, those stores are going to be telling us and telling people, in no uncertain terms; the figures will show it, you can't hide from that.

The speed with which we'll promote people and promote people from within the business says a lot. Wherever we possibly, possibly can, it's better to have someone that understands Carphone Warehouse than understands the technicalities of the job. So the head of HR in the UK used to be one of our district managers, he didn't know anything about HR when he started the job but he understood exactly the culture of Carphone Warehouse and the people who worked within it, and we hired in someone that knows HR to help. So within the organization anybody feels, almost, that they can go anywhere and do anything. At times it's dangerous, at times we create what I call, the 'Carphone Warehouse greenhouse': in our world there's never a frost and there's never anything nasty that ever happens to you, and the people that you talk to are genuine and sincere and want to help you. So we have made some mistakes where we'll promote someone quite quickly into a role where they're dealing with the outside world and they're not ready for the horrors of what people are really like.

I talk to lots of people, I send lots of emails and send very chatty emails to all the people in the company on this is what's going on, etc, this is great, this is not so great, we're trying to do this. I talk to people a lot. I think sometimes the most productive time you have is when you're somewhere in the businesses with your bum perched on the edge of a desk just chatting to people about what's going on.

We basically have a very childlike dream really, we absolutely fervently believe that if you have to buy a mobile phone, there is nowhere better, no organization that will care more about it than we do. So it's a mystery to us really why anyone buys a phone anywhere else and until everyone buys their phone from Carphone Warehouse, we won't really give up. And there's an absolute passion and missionary feeling within the organization; why on earth would anybody buy a phone anywhere else?

I think the other thing is that you have to try and break down hierarchy. Everybody must feel that everybody's got their sleeves rolled up and everyone is fighting for the same thing. It was fascinating when we bought Tandy; you could not have picked two organizations that were more different in their cultures. We merged our warehouse into their warehouse in Birmingham just before Christmas, October time, and it was a disaster it just didn't work and there was chaos. They sat behind reports and people were saying these figures can't be right. No one ever drove to the warehouse and looked round it. The view was it would be better by Easter, and this was October – we couldn't afford to wait until then. We said there's no point in managing stores if the stores don't get the right stock. So some of the directors, area managers and heads of sales went to Birmingham and ran the warehouse. The people that worked in the warehouse, who worked for Tandy, could not believe that the bosses were coming in and were driving pallets down the place, and shifting phones, and packing them up and making the whole thing work. And through this attitude of 'it's got to be fixed, we've got to make it work', we solved the problem. We didn't really realize how much we needed to do it at the time but we completely won over all the people that worked in that side of the business. It's this thing I come back to again and again: we're all in it together, we've got to do it for the customers.

Roger Taylor
Chief Financial Officer

If you want to deliver a complexity of services to the business and you want a business which can introduce propositions quickly, then you need a financial and IT team which are innovative and can understand the business dynamics. I think the culture here is good because the back-office functions, if I can call it those, are well attuned to the front-office proposition. So we have our own

We actually have screens around the building displaying our current trading performance literally updated on a 15-minute basis

IT development facility here, we effectively develop everything in house, that undoubtedly helps: it's easier to describe to our own people what we're trying to achieve than trying to describe that to a third party.

You need people who clearly are enthusiastic and keen but there's undoubtedly a young culture here and I think it's important to try not to mismatch people in what can be a very challenging environment. I think some people could find the environment quite intimidating, it is for the sort of people who are very keen to get on with it, are very enthusiastic and energetic, and if you don't meet these criteria you won't fit into Carphone Warehouse.

The way we remunerate people is totally in line with our customer proposition. Store sales executives are not paid any more for selling one network compared to another, which is very consistent with our impartial proposition. You cannot convince our sales consultants to push one product more than another, even though at times I would rather see, from a pure financial short term, one particular product being sold more than another on a different network.

What's also interesting is the culture and openness of financial information. We actually have screens around the building displaying our current trading performance literally updated on a 15-minute basis. People can understand how we're performing. I think that level of openness is good – people should understand how we're performing and that's a great motivation for people. One other thing I think is different in the culture here compared to most other companies, is what they call a 'control meeting'. On a Monday afternoon, following the previous week's trading, a full financial pack, together with non-financial data, connection numbers, levels of repairs, dropped call rates etc, all the KPIs of the business covering the entire performance of the previous week will be discussed. So we're not waiting six or seven weeks before making decisions. If you wait for your monthly management accounts to come out two or three weeks after month end, you're making decisions on things that have actually happened as long as six or seven weeks prior. I think what we're doing is making decisions on a weekly basis and the business is run on a live operating culture.

We're a business geared towards providing subscription contracts to the networks, which is a higher-value customer to the network. The business has built by providing network operators with high-value customers who are a lower credit risk to them and who spend more. That is why they like dealing with Carphone Warehouse and therefore they are able to provide us with better, more interesting propositions to the consumer. It's important that you understand what your suppliers are actually looking for in business and if you can provide them with what they want and the relationship, then the financial returns come much more easily.

Simon Nicholas

European Training and Development Officer

We invest four times the average amount on training compared to any other retailer. There's a lot of emphasis placed upon induction, training and equipping you with the knowledge and skills you require. You can't even greet the customer until you've been through two weeks of intensive training and passed the strict assessment. Then there is ongoing support and training both in-store via the intranet and off job in workshops. The one thing that enables us to be successful is our values and culture. In previous training roles, where I've been often trying to introduce programmes, it just hasn't worked and it's mainly because the culture was wrong. The approach we have here, whatever we're delivering, be it training on Personal Digital Assistance or management development, is 'let's go back to the core premise of what we're about, who we're about and what's our goal and that's about being a place where people unquestionably come for simple, impartial advice about mobile communications'. Everything we do is values orientated.

It's not about telling people, but encouraging people, so training courses are more like workshops. If I give you an example, one of the initiatives we've introduced is called 'Maximise'. Originally we were looking at formalizing how we manage people's performance, but we were uncomfortable about going down the route of organizations which create a folder and a form and have regular reviews and meetings. So the approach we took was to establish Maximise as a branded concept and say 'look at how it is aligned with who we are as a business' through a series of events, communications, meetings and workshops – first with the senior management team, then through area managers, to branch managers and now the sales execs. We didn't want to draw a very fine, straight line which people had to walk down. What we wanted to do was to create boundaries within which we expect people to operate but allow people to have the personality to do it their way.

We're a customer-service organization. The critical people who make sure that our propositions and our customers are satisfied are the sales execs themselves. They're the most important people and then everything filters back from that, and whenever Charles draws the organizational chart, he's the one right at the bottom. People within our stores are rewarded very well in commissions. The other side to reward is through recognition and progression. If we look at our managers, all of them are promoted from within and sometimes very quickly.

I think one of the things that is most distinctive about us is role modelling. It's making sure that the people delivering the message understand that it's not what they say, it's how it's delivered that's more important. There is a real desire for people to seek their own training and, as a training manager, there are loads of things that go on in this business that I only find out about after the event. There's no issue with that because they're aimed at what we're trying to achieve and I'm not precious about who is doing the training. Getting better and equipping each other to get better is core to the business; it makes my job easier if nothing else.

15

More than any other football club, or perhaps even any other sports personality or club, Manchester United has become synonymous with global branding. Its record of success in the 1990s includes five FA Cups, six Premiership titles, a European Cup Winners Cup and a Champions League title.

But it is not merely the club's record of success, it is also the style and ethos the brand is associated with which draws on a heritage of stylish, exciting and glamorous football. The culture at the club is extremely strong, focused around creating success on the pitch and an understanding of the values that have made it great.

The strength of the brand has enabled it to extend into merchandising overseas, financial services and its own digital TV channel.

15

Peter Draper

Group Marketing Director

Thousands of people have gravitated towards Manchester United and become fans over the years, all for different reasons I guess. Some come via their dad, because their dad is a fan, some because they're born somewhere fairly close to here, a vast number of people come to us as a result of the power of the media. The reason we've got so many fans in Singapore or Malaysia or Thailand or Scandinavia is because a game a week was broadcast to those marketplaces back in the early 1970s, a time when we were very successful, so people have grown up with Manchester United in far-flung places. Since then we've managed to maintain a lot of the relationships with those fans and build on them. The good thing, unlike pop groups, is that football fans tend not to change their allegiance as to whom they are going to support. So once they 'are one', it's up to Manchester United to look after that fan's interest and work with that, knowing that these people have a special relationship with us. The fans don't up and away like you would leave a bad pint of lager. That's how customers treat normal brands; they don't treat football brands like that, and we're very lucky in that respect.

I think Manchester United stands for excitement and flamboyance, a certain sense of style in the way we play and, of course, success. The will and desire to be successful drives everything and I think that, in that respect, we are a different kind of organization.

We're in the sports business clearly but we're in the entertainment business as well. What I talk about is being in the 'escapology business'. Billionaires to dustbin men can come here or engage with Manchester United and escape from whatever it is they do day-to-day. There are a lot of people that would swap their place, whatever their place in society, for one brief moment in time to score a goal at the Stretford End. The difference for us in comparison with other football teams is that we have 50 million people around the world who would do that. So we've got passion, we've got affinity and we've got loyalty but we've also got reach. It's a major difference.

Success drives us. The standards are set on the pitch. On the football side, our success rate is very high so we need to be as successful in the way we manage the business, which helps support the team. All our resources go back into regenerating the product to the highest calibre. A lot of people don't like talking about football clubs as businesses – but we do. Our job is to take the best elements of Manchester United and market them to millions of fans, millions of people. The money goes back primarily to the welfare of the core business.

The team is the demonstrable part of the brand. The football team is at the centre of the club and surrounding that is the rest of the business. So it's not two separate circles, it's a target and a bull's-eye. What I see is the team at the centre of the business and the customers at the centre of our thinking around that.

'Uncommon Practice' at Manchester United

Players are clearly a visual identifier for the brand. You don't get any better visual identifier for this brand than Sir Bobby Charlton, George Best, Denis Law, Peter Schmeichel, Eric Cantona, David Beckham or Sir Alex Ferguson. Those are the visible signposts and represent, in the most vibrant form, the core of the business called Manchester United.

We put in a lot of effort to communicate what that means to the people in the business. We say 'this is who we are, this is what we stand for and this is how we go about our business'. I think that, generally speaking, sport has treated customers pretty poorly because they've had this 'kidnap mentality'. Somebody has given you their heart and soul and it's been easy to say 'thank you very much, we'll just take that and not give much back'. I think we've changed dramatically in the last few years and now understand the need to answer to our customers and respond to their wants and needs.

It's quite a difficult job. But it is one of responsibility. The responsibility is to market to fans without being over exploitative. They have given us their hearts and their minds at some point in time and said 'I want to be a Manchester United fan', and then along comes some sort of mammoth machine and says we're going to market to you. So there's a real sense of responsibility and doing the right things for our fans is what occupies most of our time these days. Actually offering to fans what they want is really important to us. We've made vast strides in the last four or five years about understanding what kind of relationships people want. Some want just a match-going relationship, that is what really turns them on. Unfortunately we've got 50 million fans; they can't do that every week, it's physically impossible because we can only seat 67,000 people here and we actually have to try to be loyal to the core fans who come here on a regular basis. We've got local, regional, national and international fans and there is actually as much passion in Singapore for the things that are nearest our centre circle (the players) as there is in Trafford. So the whole brand mix, in terms of nurturing the continued relationship between the club and its fans, is complicated.

Our vision is to be the most pioneering football club in the world. Not to be the biggest, greatest or richest but to be the most pioneering. We're an interesting business; we've got over 500 full-time staff and a £130 million turnover or thereabouts. Small business – huge brand. In terms of market capitalization value, we've been as high as $1 billion. We're not at that level today but that's the way the market is. The brand credentials are stronger, we're doing the right things to protect the brand, particularly when it comes to the relationship with customers.

We've probably got 12, 13, 14 different kinds of businesses here: a financial services business; a merchandising and licensing business; a catering and conference business; we've got an events business; and we've got a media business (because we own a piece of television, a radio station, two monthly magazines, a website). If you start breaking it down it's quite an interesting business and actually getting people to work across the business, knowing what the end goal is, is very challenging.

We've got a good relationship on the playing side of the club; there is more understanding today that there is a requirement for us to be business oriented. We have a good dialogue with the manager and the players about responsibility to fans and customers, and they do a great deal of work to try and engender that relationship. They do it on match days, on non-match days and in charitable situations to develop a certain rapport for the club with its constituent parts. When players join us we bring them up to speed pretty quickly as to the kind of things they can expect at Manchester United because it is a different environment. They might be used to fan frenzy somewhere else, but nothing in comparison with here. Anybody who has come from a different team will tell you after 12 months 'well I thought they were a big club but I didn't realize they were this big and I didn't realize how complex it was'. We know what the players are here for, primarily they're here to play and train and rest, that's what enables us to get the product out on the field, but there are other things that we want them to do. We know that they become a visual manifestation of the brand.

Manchester United is constantly evolving. We like to be at the forefront, but we don't necessarily need to be on the extreme. The important thing, and I really do mean this, is to work with your customers. I don't care whether you're in the airline business or the sports goods business, you really have to think about the customer in the first instance and then develop products and services that are meaningful to them, because otherwise you're dead in the water. I think football has got so much to learn from other industries. But I think in the final analysis you've got to look to the football field and say teamwork is everything.

Have we got the greatest players in the world man for man? Well some people would argue with that I guess. Do we have the work ethic and the team structure to be able to overcome any inadequacies? Yes we have. That's the thing that runs through the team, the ability to be a team. And that's very important in any organization.

Management have got to embrace change and bring people to the party who are willing to work in a team environment – more and more so today otherwise some other team, somewhere else, will kick you off the park – metaphorically speaking.

Paddy Crerand

Former Player

My first experience of United was, like lots of young people in Glasgow at that particular time in the 1950s, the 'Busby babes'. I knew about Manchester United prior to Matt Busby becoming manager but that was the first thing that struck me – the Busby Babes: this great team of young players of 19/20 years of age. How could a team get all these young players all at the same time? And they were all particularly great players. Then the aircraft accident happened which always stays in my memory. I know exactly where I was when that plane crash happened in Munich.

'Uncommon Practice' at Manchester United

Most employees are dedicated Manchester United fans

Premier League contract to maintain international presence

Two monthly magazines

Three-player rule for promotional material to protect individual players

Relationship marketing across 50 million fans: local, regional, national, international

Youth teams play all over the world

Select sponsors with complementary values

Create total customer experience at matches

The atmosphere in those days was fantastic. You used to get magnificent crowds. Once the club started getting a little bit of success, the crowds started pouring in. Then George Best came on the scene. He was probably the number one attraction in Britain, off the field as well as on it, at that time. He was the one everybody wanted to see play for Manchester United – because he was a magnificent footballer. People flock from everywhere to see the likes of George Best.

I'll tell you what the club stands for – attacking football. They play football going one way. They love to attack – and it's the kind of football that people love to watch. I think that was the big attraction. And then, when you have great players as well, like United have always had down through the years, you get publicity everywhere – all over the world. I was over in Kuala Lumpur, Bangkok and Singapore when United were there three months ago – I have never seen anything like it in my life. The crowds – that fanaticism for Manchester United – it was just absolutely crazy! It was very difficult for me to explain to anybody unless you had actually been there. Crazy – how can 35,000 people turn up to watch you training? If I'd have known that before I'd have been bloody selling tickets.

Today if you're a footballer – the likes of Beckham and Giggs and Roy Keane – you are as well known in the Far East as in the UK. Television has been a great factor as well – people can switch on Sky television and CNN and can see things you would have never dreamt of seeing 30 years ago. It started in the '60s. Invariably 'Match of the Day' on a Saturday night was Manchester United. We were always the team because of Best and Charlton and Nobby Stiles and people like that.

I think Matt Busby was way ahead of his time. He introduced boxes into football grounds. For people to sit down and have a meal and watch the football match – that was unheard of! He wanted his team to be the best. Sometimes a team would play a match at Old Trafford and United might win 1– 0 and it wouldn't be attractive to watch. He would get very angry about it. 'The public have not come to watch this! They want to be entertained – that's what it is all about. If you enjoy it then the crowd out there watching must enjoy it as well'. There is a big relationship between the crowd, fans and the team. You had to play well and keep the fans happy. I think sometimes that teams go out and bore their fans because they think that if it gets them a result, it doesn't matter. That was never the Manchester United way.

It has never been Alex Ferguson's way either. It has carried on. For example, when the club travels on a plane, they wear a shirt, tie and blazer. Everybody wears the same. You don't see Manchester United travelling in a tracksuit or anything likes that – they look real smart. Matt Busby used to say: 'You're not only playing for Manchester United, you're also representing the people of Manchester'. Alex is exactly the same. I have seen Alex in action believe me! I've seen one kid who didn't have his tie on properly and, dear me, I just pushed my tie up to make sure mine was all right.

I know when Alex Ferguson came to Manchester United the first thing he did was read the history of the club. He read everything that he could possibly get hold of about Manchester United.

15

Manchester United has always had its own way of doing things. For example, everything was done for the players – all you had to do was perform. You worked hard in training but there was nothing behind the scenes that wasn't done to support you. All you had to do was turn up! You were looked after, you were given the best of everything. The biggest problem I had when I stopped playing football was turning up at an airport without my passport! A lot of players would probably say the same because the club took your passport at the start of the season and gave you it back at the end of the season. All you had to do then was turn up at the airport. The way you were treated, and the football you played, made being part of Manchester United special.

I think the sooner a lot of fans out there realize that this is a business the better. Because if you are in the business world, you can get the best – if you don't run the business well, you're not going to get the best. The business has got to be right to afford the best. The majority of people who work at United will certainly be fans. They probably get a great feeling saying to somebody 'I work at Manchester United', because it's got that magical ring about it and the magical name Manchester United. You know how when sometimes someone walks into a room and there's a reaction. Well, Manchester United has that.

Wilf McGuiness

Former Player

The secret of Manchester United is down to the football, the way they want the players to play football, and the way they've looked after the young players. Matt Busby brought young players through and so has Sir Alex Ferguson. It's a combination of bought players and young home-grown players that has been the success of Manchester United. The bought players came in with their ideas, the home-grown players were taught loyalty and team spirit and provided the bonding for the players who came in.

It starts at the top with Sir Alex Ferguson. He realizes players can make mistakes, but if they let the club down in some way he lets them know. He puts the club first in other words. I don't think other managers look at it that way, because they're not there long enough. It's a family club, that's what they want it to be, you have arguments and fall outs, but in the end you all belong to the one family. I think that's what came over when I was there and whilst Sir Alex Ferguson has been there. The players pull together, that happens in most clubs, of course, but I think it happens more at Manchester United because they stay quite a bit longer usually. Certainly the manager and the staff do, so there is a feeling of growing up together like a family.

Marketing has come into its own in recent years. They've looked at it and worked hard at it. Manchester United was the first English team in Europe and so in the European competitions. We send youth teams all over the world. People can see a team from Manchester United, from Malaysia to Malta. I think that helps marketing tremendously. Matt Busby would go to meet the supporters whenever there was an opportunity to do so. Sir Alex Ferguson was at a function in London recently. They wanted to honour him and say thank you, so he put himself out to attend.

In order to be successful, a club has to perform not only on the field, they've also got to provide an all round experience, the trip itself, because people come from so far to Old Trafford. It's all the other things like the hospitality side, you know how many people come and have meals at the ground? We're talking about 4,500. So they've got to be well treated and Manchester United do it better than any other club. We get players to walk around and be seen and sign autographs, that sort of thing. The hospitality side is the area where we have got to be spot on and make a really wonderful day out for the people. That's what we do better than the others. It's definitely a complete experience.

Harrah's

16

Harrah's is the US market leader in the gaming industry. It has brought a level of professionalism and attention to the customer experience that has set new standards, not only for the industry but across the States, being ranked first among the top 100 US companies that use IT to build customer relationships. The acronym that Harrah's uses to summarize its brand proposition is 'focus' which captures the whole approach the organization takes to running its 25 casinos. The organization has a clear and unwaivering view of its most profitable customers and uses sophisticated processes to recognize them and reward them for their loyalty. This same philosophy holds true for its employees too.

The leaders of Harrah's clearly understand the link between employee satisfaction, customer satisfaction and profitability, and measure this constantly by investing in processes and products that have the highest impact on customers. The organization is very focused too in acquiring new companies, using its company values as the criteria to determine a good fit with its brand. When it does make an acquisition, Harrah's moves quickly to ensure that the customer experience is aligned with the Harrah's brand.

16

Philip Satre

Chairman and Chief Executive Officer

Harrah's has a very strong link to the legacies of our founder, Bill Harrah. The company had built a reputation for integrity, for treating its customers and employees well, for offering high-quality products and for innovation. And it was the first to focus on the slot customer experience and the first to reward the customer for loyalty through an innovative programme that has evolved into a very sophisticated database and electronically administered loyalty programme. Bill Harrah built showrooms in the late 1950s and early '60s when most people were still just operating out of small cabarets. He recognized the value of restaurant and hotel experiences that created a more rounded resort and entertainment experience.

I'm not leading this company today based on a rigid, unchanging template, but there is a heritage and legacy that has applicability today. Harrah's will always have a high-quality product fashioned to serve our target customer base, with rooms and restaurants and entertainment experiences that create a sense of comfort for the guest. To me, it is all one seamless approach to the business. Know who your customer is and focus on him or her. Recognize what others have overlooked – that the slot customer is a very valuable customer. Focus on your employees and your customer experience. Make it an entertainment experience. Reward your customers for being loyal to you. Create the right product. Do it all with integrity. What makes us successful is that we include all these elements.

Another part of our brand – a part of what we stand for today – is the reputation of putting a high value on employees. Our 401 (k) programme, for example, is richer than anybody else's in the industry. We create an environment that empowers employees to satisfy the customer and make the customer experience as strong as possible. The focus is on the employee creating an entertainment experience for the customer.

When I think about how we're going to make decisions in this company, I reflect on our values and how a decision fits into them. I try to make decisions that allocate capital and human resources toward things that are value-based. The decision to spend the money to develop a reward system that is seamless for your customers across all properties was value-based. We promised we were going to reward loyalty, but we wouldn't be able to fulfil that promise in the new era of multiple casinos without investing in a technology that allows us to seamlessly track the customers' play and then reward them.

I remember considering a decision 12 years ago to acquire a company in the lottery industry. It was a very attractive opportunity. But we said, 'Where does that fit with our values? There's no relationship with the customer. We don't know who they are. Yes, it's the gambling industry, but it isn't what we stand for'. We ultimately said, 'This isn't going to fit'. We declined to go forward even

'Uncommon Practice' at Harrah's

Employee reward programme based on service-delivery scores

Pre-shift meetings to focus on service and share best practice

Focus training for all new recruits

Service training for all property employees

Total rewards customer loyalty programme

though it was very attractive financially. To me, that is an example of how you conclude what you're going to do, how you're going to run the business. I get asked by our young management types and MBA interns, 'How do you make the decision of how you're going to allocate resources? And what is the difference between leadership from company to company?' And I reply, 'Without putting a value statement on one leader's being better than another, the difference is how they allocate resources. Do they allocate resources to create an employee environment that fits with what they want? Do they allocate resources to create the product they want?' There are a lot of ways to make money. You can cut back on employee benefits and training programmes and you can reduce the quality of the product you build. You can ignore loyalty and say, 'We'll just wean them for all we can get and, once they're dissatisfied, we'll find the next sucker'. All of those are leadership decisions that reflect the values you think your company stands for.

You have to continuously reinforce at the senior corporate level what we stand for, how we want this business to be operated, what the leaders' roles are in carrying that out. You have to reward people who understand that and execute well, and try to convince people who have the talent but don't understand it to learn. And if they can't or if they're unwilling, then we have to move them out because we don't want our reputation and our image to be fashioned by an individual whose values are different from ours.

We don't run our business based on personal image. We do things in the image of our brand and what we stand for. We need to be stewards of that. There's room for innovation, for people to suggest improvements or that there is a sacred cow that needs to be eliminated. But ultimately we have to continuously reinforce at the senior corporate level what we stand for, how we want this business to be operated, what their role is in carrying that out.

One of the major hurdles we had to cross when we decided we were going to become a consolidator was, 'How will these acquisitions fit into our culture?' We left Rio and Showboat as separate brands, but in most cases we decided to convert to the Harrah's brand. The Harrah's Las Vegas property was operated outside the Harrah's brand for a long time. In 1990, we converted it to Harrah's. We had to invest capital to bring it up to a product level the customer would expect as a Harrah's property. We went back later and put $200 million more in because the feedback was, 'You put the Harrah's name on there, but you haven't done all the things you need to to make it a Harrah's'. We hadn't converted the experience to the brand.

The toughest lesson from the acquisitions is that you can't convert their original culture by conscripting existing management. They have an investment in the past. It's hard to get people to set aside the values they used in running the business and convince them to embrace Harrah's values. That's asking too much of the senior leadership that built what's there. Whether they are really smart, really good people or not, you have to change them out. But we've had some outstanding experiences in moving a leader from an acquired property to another Harrah's property where they can flourish with an existing infrastructure.

16

Well-trained, well-compensated, motivated, capable and satisfied employees will create satisfied customers

Communicating over and over again is the first step in bringing employees to Harrah's from other companies. Second, if we're trying to change behaviour and attitude, we look at the way people are rewarded and compensated so they understand if they do what we want them to do, they'll see higher levels of customer satisfaction, better communication among departments, growth in their own careers. The thing we try to sell more than anything else to employees, and I think we've been successful at it, is that the adoption of our culture and our approach will give them greater rewards, whether it's in their career development because of our willingness to train and develop individuals or with the compensation we're willing to offer. One consequence of loyal employees is that you have people who've been in their jobs for long periods. You have to be sensitive to their tendencies at times to become complacent or less energized about their jobs and the business. Some are unwilling to recognize why we're instituting certain changes. So you can have a continuous change process occurring while you're trying to reinforce core values.

Our core strategy is customer intimacy – focusing on the customer. That is not to say we can ignore product; we cannot. That is not to say we can ignore cost efficiencies; we cannot. The market won't let us. Our customers won't let us. We don't say we are a product innovator and that you're going to have the very best product experience at every Harrah's property on a relative basis. We don't compete that way. We also don't compete on being the low-cost provider. However, if we have a competitor which is a very good low-cost provider and the difference between their price and ours is great, the customer is going to be influenced. Then we may have to focus on cost because I want the customer to say, 'I'll pay more for Harrah's, but don't force me to pay twice as much for Harrah's'. It's the same thing with products. We want to be the leader in customer experience, not casino architecture. I think we've accomplished that. But it's a continuous challenge. If our margins get too tight and our costs are too low, then we're probably eroding our brand strategy on either the product or the customer experience.

It's very clear in my mind that there is a service-profit chain operating. Well-trained, well-compensated, motivated, capable and satisfied employees will create satisfied customers. I emphasize capable because it's not just a matter of happiness. Happy employees don't create the environment. It is capable, satisfied employees – meaning they have the tools, the understanding and the training to deliver something to the customer – who create satisfied customers. Focusing only on happy employees is a short-lived experience, because if you're not successful in achieving customer satisfaction, the business enterprise doesn't succeed. Morale isn't going to be high if the business isn't succeeding.

We're in the chance business, as we like to say, but there's no reason to leave the customer's experience to chance. Whether it's identifying which casino to visit, checking into the hotel, buying into the game, getting the jackpot payoff, being served at a restaurant or checking out of the hotel, it can't be left to an execution that doesn't have very tight process. The way we approach this is to script at the corporate level very heavily. We script the marketing process. We script the human resource recruitment, training, compensation and benefit process very heavily. We script the hotel experience because we think that's a core experience. We script the restaurant and slot experiences for the same reasons.

Our key challenge is to continue to have healthy, profitable growth. It's important to our shareholders, but it's also important to our employees and our management to feel as if they're part of something vibrant. We want to do that in an environment in which it can be achieved primarily through organic growth and consolidation. Our toughest decisions are how we use our resources for consolidation or organic growth, whether it's through our loyalty programme or adding hotel rooms and restaurants and new features to our properties.

We're now at more than 44,000 employees. We have a key management meeting every year. The first time I went to a key management meeting in this company we had less than 50 people. At the last, we had 230 people. You used to be able to pick up the daily financial reports and absorb what happened the day before at four or five properties. Now we're managing the complexity of a large organization with 25 properties in 12 states while continuing to have the feel of a vibrant company that cares about each individual customer, that cares about each individual employee and that respects what we stand for. That's a challenge.

Gary Loveman

President and Chief Operating Officer

When I came to Harrah's, the problem and the opportunity confronting the company was that the general level of service delivery in the gaming industry was mediocre at best. There was no manifest loyalty to casino companies by their customers. We seek to have an experience with our guests that is truly memorable, so they are favourably disposed to Harrah's and don't shop their next visit among the several providers that exist in all our markets.

In our business, service is truly the driver of profitability. I wanted our employees to believe that service drives profits. If we got better at service, I would give them a big slug of money. And that employee-reward programme has been very successful so far. Also, there had been no active brand development. Because we are the only truly national casino operator, it behoves us to pursue a branding strategy. So we used branding approaches with the goal of identifying the joy and critical emotions of gaming with Harrah's. When you see our logo, you think of what it feels like when you're dealt an ace and you're waiting to see if the next card is a 10. Or when the first two wheels come up seven and you're waiting to see if the third one's going to be a seven. The term we use for it is 'exuberantly alive'. It's what our customers tell us they feel like.

One of the things I've always found most fascinating is that there is considerable transparency to the worth of a customer. We know exactly how much a customer is worth and treat him accordingly.

16

God created all people equally; She did not create all customers equally

I've said to our employees, 'God created all people equally; She did not create all customers equally'. So we treat great customers better than we treat middle-level customers, better than we treat modest-level customers. And the differences are obvious to those who aren't getting the better treatment. The more active a gamer you are, the stronger the incentive to be a part of our Total Rewards programme because the programme disproportionately rewards better players.

The critical thing I talk to our employees about is the notion that when you go to work, your job over the next 8 to 10 hours is to see to it that five or six people finish the day with a relationship with Harrah's they didn't have when they started. At the end of the day, there has to have been a bond built between you and a handful of guests to have made that a successful shift.

We have people meet before shifts to focus on the quality of service, the lessons learned, the best practices. And the effect is reflected in the extraordinary service scores this year. Last year in the first quarter, three properties improved service enough to qualify for the Reward Programme for employees. In the first quarter of this year, 13 have.

Marilyn Winn

Senior Vice-President, Human Resources

Gaming is a very personal service business. We hire and motivate people to demonstrate their personality when they deliver the service. We have our Focus training for every new hire, be they in the kitchen, a direct customer contact person, a supervisor, a manager, a VP or general manager. At Harrah's, all our property employees attend a service-training programme in which we talk about what our guests want.

We have more stringent assessment and interview standards at Harrah's than other companies. In 1999 our turnover rate was about 45 percent. We have moved that rate down through focusing on pre 90-day turnover. Our goal is to achieve a 10 percent improvement in turnover. If you aim at the 'quick quits', the rest of the turnover will take care of itself.

I used to tell my staff, 'We are like a stained glass window. Valets over here, food and beverage here, tables and slots all working together to create a great picture in the customer's mind. If any part of our team has performed poorly, that's the piece the customer is going to remember. So think of yourselves as a team creating one impression on the customer'. I am less interested in finding the individual star because they're hard to find and they're hard to reward, and they're a challenge to manage. The teamwork element is what we're really striving for.

We are working towards the adoption of a common leadership language. We've defined leadership as identifying your vision, aligning systems to achieve the vision, and then inspiring employees. We have taken our high-potential managers, as well as our senior leaders, through a development programme on what leadership means, what it looks like, and how to put the action steps into place. We often start our training and development programmes with the concept of the service-profit chain. And we use that concept in our supervisory training. We have four regional training centres where new supervisors attend training within the first month of being promoted or hired. The reason for this is important: we don't want a poor-performing supervisor practising on our employees. We want new supervisors to learn performance management first.

Harrah's is the only company I know where everyone can earn a bonus. And it doesn't matter if you are front of the house or work in a non-customer contact position. Property bonuses are based upon customer-satisfaction scores.

John Bruns

Director, Corporate Customer Satisfaction Assurance

We have a three part strategy for success. First is the service culture at Harrah's. When I joined the company, I went out and talked to my customers who included all of the general managers and the leadership teams. I went out and said, 'Tell me about the customer-satisfaction programme. Tell me what you like, tell me where you think the challenges are'. I received a great deal of input, as you can imagine. As I gathered input, synthesized it, and played it back to them, we did a lot of 'what if'. What if it would look like this? What if it looked like that? As we designed it at one property, I'd take it to the next property the next day or the next week. We just kept moving it from property to property, saying, 'Would this work for you?' And they'd improve on it.

Second is the service process. What we're after with the service-delivery system is that we can be friendly, helpful but we need to make sure that the customer is also in a state of readiness to have a great moment of truth. As an example, if you waited in line 20 minutes and here's your smiling, bright, happy cashier who's ready to serve you but you are mad, what is the quality of that interaction? And we own that. We own that because you waited in line. It was our service-delivery system that caused that wait, because we go out and market to you, we attract your business, you come, and if we can't handle the volume, shame on us. The third part is the alignment, the roles and responsibilities. Each employee at Harrah's has a specific role and a responsibility not only to the service culture but also to the continuous improvement cycle.

John Lewis

17

The John Lewis Partnership is one of the most highly respected retailers and the largest department store group in the UK. It is also Britain's biggest and longest-surviving example of worker co-ownership, with over 54,000 partners and a constitution originating in 1929; it is viewed by many as offering a blueprint for a more humane way of doing business.

With 26 department stores and 136 supermarkets in its Waitrose chain, turnover to January 2001 was over £4 billion. For 75 years its slogan 'never knowingly undersold' has summarized its dedication to delivering customer value, characterized by a very distinctive, polite service. The commitment to the democracy of the partnership is critical to understanding the sustained success of the business.

Sir Stuart Hampson

Chairman and Chief Executive

The John Lewis Partnership has always operated from a set of values. We are unique amongst companies in having a written constitution which was first drawn up in 1929. When I became chairman I decided that I wanted to bring it up to date, because it was expressed in a number of documents written by lawyers and was totally inaccessible to the majority of our people. The very process of saying 'let us bring it up to date and let us do it in the spirit of our business', that is to say democratically, was a reaffirmation of our values by all our now 54,000 partners. The process, which took us about two years, was enormously invigorating because it crystallized many of the things that people knew about, and felt instinctively, but in simple words they could understand.

The constitution highlighted four specific constituents that were important to the value of the business. First of all, and most significant in our terms, was the relationship of employees because our business is formed on the notion that labour employs capital, not capital employing labour, and that is a fundamental difference between our business and a conventionally constituted company. We're a PLC in formal company terms, but all our shares are owned by a trust so employees are beneficial owners of the company. We believe that the 54,000 people working in this business should know what's going on and not just be told through a spin-doctoring process. If I can give an example of the effect of that, in my first year as chairman we announced the worst partnership bonus (profit sharing) since the Korean War. The response to it was wholly positive. Our partners knew the economy was going through a recession and throughout the year we'd been communicating; sharing figures, both in terms of our sales and the impact on the bottom line. Sharing of power follows because we believe partners should have a sense of responsibility – to improve the business as well as a right to benefit from its success.

Co-ownership means sharing the challenges as well as the rewards. We've just gone through a process in the department stores of looking at how we can extend the trading window. Many of our shops used to trade five days a week, some traded six days a week. Now longer trading hours meant everyone changing their hours of work and in many cases being asked to extend their contracts to trade on Sundays. Instead of management saying 'this is what will happen', we have been going through a process of involving every single person who works in the shops and then making the decision by an elective body of partners. Every single proposal has been carried – it's trusting partners to actually participate in difficult decisions. We deal with major issues that will affect the competitiveness of our business. The managing director of each shop examines the possibilities and takes a very firm lead, but then we allow democratic ownership to operate.

It is about sharing of knowledge, sharing of power then finally sharing profit, with our staff rather than with outside shareholders. The board decides how much we need to retain in the business for future expansion and investment, all the rest goes to our partners. We do that as an equal

'Uncommon Practice' at John Lewis

Constitution for partnership

54,000 partners

'Never knowingly undersold' policy

Equal percentage profit share scheme

Customer focus groups

Buyers visit every store once or twice a year

Full-time employment policy

Six-month sabbatical on full pay for 25 years' service

Full information policy for all partners

Total integrity with suppliers

Committed to being good neighbours in society

---

more...

percentage of pay to every single person. Last year the bonus was 10 percent, so I got 10 percent of my pay, a part-time sales assistant got 10 percent of his or her pay. If we say that pay reflects the contribution you make to the business, why should there be successive layers of extra bonuses the higher you go up in the business? You want to incentivize people throughout the business, so our principle is to get the pay right as an accurate contribution of each individual's input into the business and then everybody gets the same percentage. We don't have pay bands, we don't have annual increments. Everyone has their pay performance judged each year according to their contribution and the bonus rests on it.

The constitution also recognizes the importance of our relationship with our customers, partly represented by our slogan 'never knowingly undersold'. It is a commitment that we are on the side of the customer and that we will go to great lengths to offer value. It says that you've no need, as a customer, to go running up and down the high street checking the prices, because we actually employ somebody to do that for you. Our aim is to say 'this is your shop which we are running on your behalf'.

The third constituency are our suppliers where we have distinct rules for total integrity dealing with them. We recognize that the success of a food chain like Waitrose depends critically on the product. We want to distinguish ourselves by providing things that customers don't see elsewhere. Therefore, we want suppliers who feel engaged with us, understand our philosophy, are prepared to share long-term prospects, and work with us. Waitrose works with farmers to understand them, to have long-term contracts with them. During the foot and mouth crisis, for example, we were in touch with all our farmers on a regular basis, they knew that we would stick with them, honouring the relationships we've had, the prices that we've agreed to. Indeed, one of the reasons for sacking the chairman, written in our constitution, is if we don't pay our bills on time! If ever a supplier makes a mistake, we will correct it for them.

The fourth constituency is the community and it was first expressed in the early constitution that we will be good neighbours in society. A very simple expression because concepts such as the environment weren't invented then, so it was in the sense that we will be well mannered neighbours. For example, if you look at Waitrose supermarkets you will not see aggressive structures that impose themselves on the local environment.

These four concepts have been the bedrock of our business for 70 years. Very frequently people, who are nervous about a business organized on these principles, will say 'but aren't you constantly meeting conflicts?' If you say the objective of management is to please the shareholder, then you're looking in the wrong direction. If you say creating shareholder value is the company's goal, even if it motivates top management, it certainly won't motivate the people on the selling floor. Why will customers say 'I really enjoy shopping at John Lewis' or 'shopping in Waitrose is such a pleasure?' It's because staff feel motivated, valued, they understand and enjoy their relationship with the customers. In Waitrose we aim to have people working there who first of all really enjoy

17

Focus on the drivers of profit, not on profit itself

talking to people and secondly who are passionate about food. If we make it an enjoyable shopping experience for our customer, our business will grow. So if we start with what we are trying to create at the front end and management focuses on those elements, then the profit flows through. If your focus is to make more profit by reducing pay, because in retailing that's your biggest cost, you have fewer people on the selling floor. The result is more stressed staff who feel that they can't deliver service. As a result, the customers go shopping elsewhere. Focus on the drivers of profit, not on profit itself.

Our people are key. That's down to recruitment and training. Getting people who are confident, who want to sell, and who are passionate about their area. I was in one of our supermarkets the other day and I overheard a conversation where one of our sales assistants was saying to a customer 'hello, I haven't seen your husband in here for a while, is he all right?' Here was a sales assistant, not talking about the product, but recognizing a customer well enough to ask after her husband. That shows the success of building a relationship and that is better than any plastic loyalty card. Most loyalty cards encourage promiscuity because customers carry a whole collection in their wallets and then shop around. Loyalty comes from people who really make a difference.

You get that by creating an atmosphere in the business. In our shops there is a clear understanding of what we're trying to achieve and that's a business which will sustain its success over a long time. Of course managers look at their profits, their costs, but we are quite clear that managing in anything other than a democratic way is unacceptable in our business. Any manager who feels that he can ignore our democratic principles, even if he feels he can produce a wonderful profit, is not acceptable. I repeat that regularly, it is very clearly understood.

For a long time now we have conducted focus groups where we invite cross-sections of the customers to tell us what we're doing right and what we're doing wrong. When we started out we found they were very difficult to get going, mainly because customers were too nice to us and didn't want to offend us, which perhaps says something about our relationship with them. We now say 'this is your opportunity and we want to know what it is that bugs you about our shops, how can we do better. Don't stroke us, tell us the things we could do better'.

Our aim is total fairness with the customer. To be on their side if anything goes wrong. The way in which we deal with instances when things go wrong is critical. It's how you recover from that situation which builds your reputation. I had an example where a man had bought a present for his wife which had a part missing. He wrote to me in some high fury so I wrote back saying 'I'm really sorry, I can imagine how disappointed your wife must be and we'll put it right as soon as we can'. I faxed it over to the manager of Peter Jones who wrote to the wife the same day saying 'Our chairman has just sent me this letter, we really are sorry and we are on to it' and passed it straight to the department manager who got the spare part and sent it round in a taxi to the customer, whereupon the customer wrote to me saying 'I give in!' I keep repeating the word 'integrity', but that is what we try to achieve.

'Uncommon Practice' at John Lewis

Above state minimum redundancy pay policy

Committees for Communication in every branch

Hardship fund

No individual perks policy

'Communications half hours' involving all partners

Two partners' newspapers, the *Chronicle* and the *Gazette*

'Free press' section on intranet to allow partners to air their views

Subsidized social and leisure facilities, such as social clubs, hotels and a fleet of yachts

I want John Lewis to be two things in the future. The destination of choice for our customers and the employer of choice for people who want to work in retailing and have the creative and individual talents that would suit our business. I deliberately state both of those because I think unless you achieve both of them you won't achieve either of them. We put a huge emphasis on full-time employment in contrast with most retailers who depend on a core of managers and part-time staff to match their varying trade pattern throughout the week. We've always recruited full-timers because we want people who want to make their career in retailing. Is also gives continuity of service to customers which is something we've always attached importance to. We want to have a pool of talent that we can promote, so the people who come in at the bottom have the opportunity to become the managers of tomorrow.

We have very considerable numbers of people who have been with us 25 or 30 years and we value them enormously. They are the bedrock of the business, they understand the values we're talking about, they live and breathe them. Anyone who's been with the business for 25 years gets a six-month sabbatical on full pay. Many of them are quite young; if you joined at 17, after 25 years you are only 42 and you have got another 20-odd years to go, so this is a chance to 'recharge the batteries' and take a fresh outlook on life to equip you for the second part of your career.

My advice for others in business is to have a clear understanding of what you're setting out to do and follow it relentlessly. It's not a recipe for complacency, because focusing on what you're trying to achieve with an understanding of changeless values enables you to look at the constantly changing environment around you and adapt. We are facing change in retailing, not just because the competitors change but because the customers' expectations change and if you are looking at that, monitoring it, thinking about it and aiming to satisfy those customer expectations and to do it within your set of values, then you can adapt and constantly lead.

Dudley Cloake

Director of Personnel

The essential ingredient in a co-owned business is to have managers who manage in a democratic fashion, who treat people as adults, give them plenty of scope, listen to what they're saying and involve them in decisions, as far as it is possible, to keep them informed. Accountability is taken to an extraordinary extent in the partnership. We're accountable to the owners of the business – our 54,000 partners. Questions come from partners at any level; there's no limitation on what they can and can't ask. One of the things that we require of our managers is the ability to handle that situation. People have to be capable of managing in an inclusive way, involving people in decisions, ensuring people are aware of what's going on.

It's traditionally a business that's found its management from within. Managers tend to stay longer compared with other businesses. It's unfashionable perhaps, but many people are happy to spend

17

Many people are happy to spend much or all of their career in the partnership

much or all of their career in the partnership. We don't have things like special bonus schemes or long-term incentive plans, share options are impossible because the capital of the business is owned by a trust, but I think the senior management here feel comfortable in a business with these values. That's what it's all about, a kind of unwritten contract with the partnership. Of course, we recruit from outside as well – I think we'd become a terribly inward-looking business if we didn't.

We don't apply psychometric testing; we've never persuaded ourselves it's a valuable tool. If I sit down with a line manager to interview someone, we both know what we're looking for because we understand the values of the business. There won't be any major disagreement about whether someone is likely to be a good cultural fit.

I'd like to think one of the things the partnership is able to offer is variety and a willingness to consider people for all sorts of different jobs; in other words to look at generic skills and see the value of these in a variety of different jobs. After all, this is a people business and managing people, motivating people is a key skill. Managing through people, being able to delegate effectively, to motivate a team, is probably the one thing they need to have. It's probably the thing they can't afford to be without.

Another difference between many other businesses and us is we try and help, to quite an extraordinary extent, people stay in the partnership. Of course, you've also got to be pretty hard-headed about it. We will do our level best to improve the performance of unprofitable businesses but if we don't think a business can really be successful long term then we have no choice but to close it, because otherwise it endangers the employment of partners generally. But if someone from a business unit that has been closed, goes for a new job in the partnership, they don't have to be the best qualified for that job. They will get it because they'll have come from somewhere where jobs have been lost. The expectation is they will be able to do it to an acceptable standard within a reasonable period, but they don't have to be the best qualified, that's the difference. Also, our redundancy pay is significantly better than the state minimum. If you make these decisions you have to recognize the fact that we're losing our co-owners, they have rights and we have duties and obligations towards them.

A business which actually sets its sights pretty high in terms of customer service can only be sustained if we have people who really like dealing with people. If you don't like people go and find something else to do. It can be damned hard work, it can be long, unusual hours but in the end it's the dealing with people and, on the whole, very agreeable people, that makes the job what it is.

Alistair McKay

Partners' Counsellor

My main role is acting as the partnership's ombudsman but I also have responsibility for the work of 13 'Committee for Communication Chairmen'. Now let me explain. Each branch has a committee for communication who can only be non-management. Committee for communication partners are elected annually by their colleagues in the branch. A committee for communication chairman runs these meetings and it really is from the heart, it's from the shop floor. There are minutes, but confidentiality is key. Any comment made at that meeting is not attributable. It could be that they are very unhappy with the day-to-day courtesy shown by management. It could be that they're fed up with a cold shop floor. If nothing's done about it, it's an ideal opportunity to bring it up with the committee for communication chairmen who have a direct line to Stuart Hampson. So they have to meet five times a year in the department stores and four times a year in Waitrose – our 54,000 partners have this direct line to the chairman and it works. It's a committee where anything they bring up is given priority to be fixed because it gets so much exposure.

The meetings occur during work hours so managers will lose those partners off the shop floor, but I haven't heard of a case yet where managers complained about that. They see it as an essential part of the communication structure and it is non-management's opportunity to voice their concerns or, indeed, praise. We call it the 'talking shop that works'. And it's two-way communication. There are often messages that Sir Stuart will want to get down to the shop floor. It may be that profits are affected by decisions that our central council has made. It may be that we need to manage expectations about the annual bonus. We want them to go out and talk over their coffee cups to their friends and we want them to communicate any feedback they get to management.

It's fair to say that most heads of branch and Waitrose branch managers go along to these meetings with a degree of apprehension because you don't know what's going to come at you. I heard a head of branch say that he thought that the committee for communication was the jewel in the partnership's democratic crown. It puts out a very strong message regarding freedom of speech and ownership of the business.

Integrity jumps out at me at John Lewis and an openness and honesty that I certainly didn't experience in any of the jobs I had previously. Consider a director getting a complimentary diary through the post from a consultancy. Now, in a lot of businesses that director would just pop it in his briefcase and take it home. At John Lewis the director declares this diary, a price is quoted and he or she will pay for the diary. That money goes into a windfall account which is controlled along with other funds by another branch committee called the committee for claims. Partners in hardship can appeal to this committee, to try and help them out with anything which can range from rent arrears to funeral bills they can't afford. That has always been the principle in John Lewis, you should not enjoy any perks the average partner can't enjoy.

THE UK'S BUSIEST HI-FI RETAILER

18

The Guinness Book of Records credits Richer Sounds, the hi-fi chain, with having the highest sales per square foot of any retailer in the world every year since 1991. The organization has achieved this remarkable result through an uncompromising focus on delivering good quality products, great value for money and employing very friendly people.

Julian Richer, the founder, is passionate about motivating his people to the extent of providing them with holiday homes, luxury cars for the weekend and trips on the company jet. He reckons all this is more than paid for by shrinkage and absenteeism rates that are less than half the industry average.

Equally remarkable, the company donates 7 percent of pre-tax profits to a wide range of charitable projects and allows staff to actively work on projects on paid leave. But this is by no means a 'soft' culture; employees are fined for poor service and the organization is as quick to demote people as it is to promote them.

Julian Richer

Chairman

It's quite clear to me what the Richer brand stands for. That is value for money in parallel with great customer service. We may not always achieve it but we're trying very hard. I can't think of one business that it doesn't apply to. Everyone wants value for money, everyone wants service. If you offer service without value then, of course, people feel they're paying extra for it; if you offer people value without service, then there is no loyalty, just hunters moving from bargain to bargain. So whether it's my bar which is packed every night, or my chain of hi-fi stores, we're still aiming to offer those two things. When I say value for money, in terms of the hi-fi stores, the value is determined by the manufacturer. A Sony hi-fi component is a fixed quality, so customer service becomes the differentiator. This is in the forefront of our minds in everything we do from the moment we recruit somebody to the training we give, to measurement of performance, then, of course, to the rewards as well, we are focusing on those two things in parallel.

If you were a member of the board, you would know this because we only promote internally. You would have it ingrained in you to the very depths of your soul. But it is not just at board level, it's in every aspect of our business. It's how long we take to answer the phone, how friendly we are when we answer the phone. This isn't a science, but we believe the more ways you measure it, the more accurate it becomes, so if I want my business to provide great service and value for money, those are the things we measure. For value for money we're doing tests twice a week in every hi-fi store in the country, we check the competition regularly, we're fanatically aggressive on price as far as the competition is concerned. In terms of customer service, we measure it in as many ways as we possibly can. We have mystery shoppers both in the store and on the phone, the call centre, on the website. I could bore you rigid on this!

I think you should never promise great customer service. I believe in underpromising and overdelivering. For example, if I invited you to come on a trip in six months' time and I kept saying how amazing it was going to be every day, by the time it happened you are going to be pretty unimpressed about it all, but if I said the day before, 'can you make up the numbers, I don't know if you are going to enjoy it or not', and we have a good time you'll say 'Wow!' It's the same in the store. It's very important not to promise service but price is a very different thing.

I want customers to really believe that they're going to get the best deal from me, and we underwrite that with a real promise, no 'ifs' and 'buts', we will beat anyone's price by up to £50. The reason for this is that it is our marketing weapon and so we need to be very, very confident. All of our marketing effort has to get across two messages, value for money and the perception of friendliness without promising great service.

Delivering great service requires you to 'keep the buzz'. Keeping the buzz relates to our colleagues, because people are not like buildings. You can put up a building and forget about it for 50 years.

'Uncommon Practice' at Richer Sounds

Only promote internally

Twice-weekly nationwide checks on value for money

Employee commission scheme

10 holiday homes for employees in the UK and Europe

Employee benefit programme

Empty-seat policy for employees on company jet

Hardship fund for employees

Richer League measurement scheme which awards a Bentley or Rolls-Royce for the weekend!

Questionnaire on all till receipts

Weekly conference call for all managers

Annual attitude survey

Monthly in-house video

Quarterly in-house magazine *The Richer Way*

Annual company outing

Mystery shopper checks

Funky art and sculpture in the head office to add fun

Morale today can be fantastic, I can change the commission scheme tomorrow and employees can all be down in the dumps. I realize that people are very delicate and we have to work on that, and we mustn't take their morale for granted. Whatever I did for them last year in terms of holiday homes and perks is soon forgotten about, they want to know what we're going to do for them this year. As an employer I don't think how can I cut my wage cost this year, I'm thinking what can I do to really excite colleagues even more this year? We place a lot of emphasis on our colleague benefits, discounts at the gym club, chiropody, etc. A couple of years ago I bought an eight-seater executive jet and we said we'll have an empty seat policy so whenever I go on a business trip, seven colleagues go with me. The irony is I've got to keep sober because I'm on a business trip, they're all getting smashed and having a wild time! So far I've taken 200 of my colleagues on the jet.

I also invest 1 percent of our profits in the hardship fund which can be used by employees if they have problems of any kind; it allows colleagues to visit my personal doctor in Harley Street, for example. What does that say to our colleagues? Firstly they've never been to Harley Street before so they've got an hour to talk about their problems rather than five minutes, secondly the doctor must be good, because he is the chairman's doctor, and I can afford to go anywhere, and thirdly the company really cares about me when I've got a problem. For what it costs me, it's the best £100 I can spend.

I'm really into loyalty and rewarding ability and therefore I don't like people coming in on a higher level. I just think if I were a young lad, who hadn't had an education and I see some smart graduate coming over me, however good they are, I'm going to feel bad. So we promote internally. I also like people having dual roles so, for example, we don't have area managers but the better managers will supervise other branches. We have a guy in charge of recruitment and training who's an ex-store manager, who worked his way up. He was demoted first of all because he wasn't up to being a manager at first. He's a wonderful, wonderful guy, he was only about 12 years old when we made him manager of the Liverpool store, then had to demote him! A lot of business associates ask 'how can you demote people?' Most organizations are terrible at demoting people, but we manage it very well. At our 'virgin seminars' where we train new recruits I stand up and say how we are quick to promote and quick to demote, I point to this guy and say 'look he was demoted and look at him now, he's a director'.

I'm not on the management board any more, but I still see every single colleague suggestion, I then ask directors for their comments. I still see all the customer correspondence, every letter that comes to the company still gets a reply signed by me. I am a figurehead for colleagues, for suppliers and for customers and that is one thing I haven't let go of.

I measure everything that moves! We have the Richer League which is a service-based measurement scheme and each month we have three winners, who each get the use of a Rolls-Royce or Bentley for the weekend. These are inner-city kids who have never been in a Bentley in their lives. They can use it to visit their old school friends, or go down to the pub or take their mother-in-law out for

You can always find excuses not to do things in life

tea, they have lots of fun with it. I don't dare to think what they get up to in the evenings, but they have lots of fun! If you're employing teenagers, you've got to focus on your target audience. It's not appropriate for all businesses, but my group of mostly young people have a wonderful time with this. I think we've had one write-off over the years, but you can always find excuses not to do things in life.

All departments in the company compete, we measure accounts and how quick they answer the phones and deal with queries, so we're not just measuring the salespeople. I believe in lots of fun and motivation things but also quite a few controls. We've got best practices we've developed over 23 years; that inevitably involves measurement to check we are maintaining those standards. So you can afford to have the fun as long as you've got the disciplines behind the scenes. That is a very, very important balance that we continually aim to get right.

My definition of culture is your perception of the organization as an employee. So for the culture to be a good, positive, happy one employees have to believe in it, and that will only come through lots of effort. At the end of the day the Bentleys cost very little, the jet is flying anyway, the holiday homes we provide cost a few thousand a year but the downside cost of having disgruntled or demotivated employees is phenomenal. It's absenteeism, labour turnover, theft, bad customer service. So I would argue that what I spend on these things is worth every penny. The turnover of Richer Sounds this year is about £85 million and we figure that retail theft in this country is about 2 percent of turnover. We believe ours is under 1 percent. So the 1 percent we are saving because our colleagues are more loyal and happier and think we are decent employers, is £850,000 a year. That difference pays for what we do.

Let's turn to the customer experience. I often say 'underpromise and overdeliver', therefore I don't mind that our stores are a little bit scruffy, because if you go into a classy store your expectations are very high, and if the service is mediocre you think 'what a rip off'. My shops are small and a little bit hectic but when you get a sales assistant that is nice to you and cares for you, you go 'Wow!' Of course, the benefit to me is that I've got small shops that are cheap, but I'm running a business and I want to keep my costs to a minimum. If you want to buy a mini-disc player that we are making a 5 percent gross margin on I can't afford 15 percent in rent. So we are benefiting our customers too.

My ambition for the Richer brand is to go into Europe quite substantially. We want to build up in Holland and if that is successful then I want to look at Germany which is a huge market. I'm doing other things which I enjoy as well as roll out my theories and philosophies to other businesses which is also very exciting. If you get a chance, go to my bar in Fulham Road called Lomo. Last night I couldn't even get in the door and that is on a Wednesday night. It's quite an interesting example because where most bar staff get £5 an hour, we are paying between £12 and £14 an hour but linked to customer service and mystery shopping scores. It's exactly the same philosophy.

Claudia Vernon

Marketing Director

The brand promise and customer service message are vital to our business; they are the same. Richer is known for providing good value for money and being friendly. If you get a customer complaining about bad service and they feel they have been 'ripped off', word soon gets around, but when customers experience good, friendly customer service and value for money products, then that is the best form of advertising any retailer can have; you can't put a price on that.

Our marketing department treats our stores as our customers. We give them the sort of service we would expect to receive in our stores. I monitor my department's performance on a weekly basis with a simple ticking box on a sheet sent back to our department with the store's weekly point of sale requirements. Our stores need the right merchandise, point of sale, adverstising and catalogues to enable them to sell to the customer – without these tools, good customer service would be hard to achieve. In addition to all the pieces the customer sees, all stores have lots of point of sale 'behind the scenes'. It is vital to remind colleagues to 'smile: you're on camera' and other fun messaging before they go onto the shop floor.

My managers are both ex-Richer Sounds store colleagues – one was a store manager and the other an assistant manager. I think that is where Richer Sounds differs from the rest of the sector. I don't have a marketing degree. Julian doesn't look for traditional qualifications in a person and is fantastic at spotting people's potential.

One other thing we do, to ensure that communications are great between the stores and the support team, is produce a monthly video. It's a very amateur production, with no editing! Julian will give an overview of the company, then all department heads will update colleagues on their progress. The marketing segment is literally like a Blue Peter video, 'this is how you make this', 'this is how this display should look', etc. This enables us to achieve continuity throughout our stores, and seeing it on video is far easier than sending out instructions (although we do back it up with a set of these as well). We also produce a quarterly in-house magazine called 'The Richer Way', which is an update on all sections of the business. It is fun and has competitions, funny photos and captions. It also gives information on any forthcoming extra-curricular activities that the company has planned like the yearly outing. We back these up with hilarious teaser posters which we put in the stores' point of sale bags to let everyone know 'not to miss out!'

Richer Sounds is about motivation. If colleagues aren't happy, then they are not going to give good customer service. Staff turnover in general is very low. In marketing departments, you would normally expect a designer to stay for 14-18 months before they felt it necessary to move on to further their portfolio. My art director has been with me six years and most of my designers stay for two to three years. I think this says a lot about they way we work as a company.

18

David Robinson

Managing Director

We would probably say that our brand is good quality products at the best possible price in a fun, customer-service-orientated environment. Not only are we giving you a great deal, but it's also a good shopping experience, so hopefully we're starting to link you into staying with us and recommending us. It's building a relationship with customers. I would much rather that our people say to customers 'Take time out, don't buy it today if you're not sure, think about it, have a coffee and come back'. Otherwise customers feel pressured and when they get their purchases home it's actually not what they wanted.

Everybody who buys from us gets a receipt, and on the edge of every receipt is a questionnaire in which we ask a few simple questions. The most important one is 'please rate the overall level of service' and it ranges from excellent to poor. If sales assistants get 'excellent' or 'very good', they're awarded with an amount of money. If they get a 'poor' or 'very poor', they're deducted some money, but that doesn't happen very often. We measure it so that we can see very clearly who's hitting the right mark and who isn't and they feel rewarded for doing so.

Last year, our average was 86 percent of customers saying that the service they'd received was either excellent or very good. This year we've said our year goal is to try and keep it over 90 percent and at the moment we're averaging somewhere between 90–92 percent which is great because we know we're not just keeping our service at a level, we're doing things to improve it and are actually driving forward.

I think it's a culture that you either sink or swim in. It's either a culture you really, really enjoy and you love it and stay a long time or you leave very quickly and I think that's always been the case. We've got lots of incentives but they're all incentives that are measured and are fair and accurate. So if you don't like being responsible for your own actions, if you don't like being rated, you're not going to stay around. The reverse of that is a culture that attracts a lot of people who feel 'I can do that, I can sell to people and be well rewarded' and if that's the kind of person you are you'll enjoy the culture that we have.

We try new things all the time. All the managers get together on a conference call on Monday mornings and not only do we talk about stores, trading weeks and figures, but if we've introduced something new it will be discussed, so we know we're going to get feedback so we can fine-tune it or change it or pull it from the stores. If we don't try things we'll never move forward and if we don't get things wrong it means we're not trying things.

There's always got to be a group of people driving the business forward. One of the things I say to the management team is we've always got to remember that the people who are out there in the

Take time out,
don't buy it today
if you're not sure,
think about it,
have a coffee
and come back

stores are paying our wages and that's the most important lesson. And we've got to be prepared to listen. We listen to them in lots of different ways. It's a very open style of management. It has to be – if you want to be at the forefront of your sector, you've got to react quickly and you've got to be prepared to listen. Our annual attitude survey has just come out and I'm delighted with the results because year-on-year we're improving some of the results and as you grow one of the things that's very difficult is having the same contact and the same communication and often is one of the first things that gets lost.

You've got to decide what your brand stands for, you have got to believe in it and you have got to communicate it. And these two things are not easy. It's easy to say this is what our brand stands for, but communicating it and believing in it are two different things. For us being in customer service means it's not good enough for me to write a memo every three months saying service levels are down, we've had a lot of complaints, we've got to do something about it. I've got to be up front, I've got to check customer service records. Julian talks about *kaizen*: it's a Japanese belief that you're always travelling along the road and you never get there. Which is why we're wary when people say 'you've got the perfect brand', well we haven't, we get it wrong and maybe for every 50 customers you speak to you can find one that we've got it wrong with. We put our hands up when we do get it wrong and say 'let's see if we can sort it out, it's no problem – how can we learn from it and improve in the future?'

The only thing that makes the brand strong is the people, and we do a lot of things for our employees that probably don't make any difference to the outside world in a marketing sense, but what these things do is to create loyalty. We get hard-working people from it we get motivated people enjoying the job that they do. For example, we've got 10 holiday homes throughout the UK and Europe, it's paying above average in the industry, it's having a hardship fund so if employees get into problems we can help them out, it's getting them medical advice if they need it, it's the whole range of what we do. The people working at Richer Sounds are the centre of Richer Sounds. Without them we haven't got Richer Sounds.

People sometimes forget that the brand is built on a very, very strong foundation of Julian. You have to have that enthusiastic figurehead driving the brand forward, because otherwise, if it's left to a group of suits in the office, you don't have a brand.

amazon.com.

19

Amazon.com is one of the most widely recognized and respected brands in the world today. The brand's clear proposition and reputation for delivering on its promise have enabled it to grow from start-up to nearly $3 billion in sales in just six years. It serves over 38 million customers in 220 countries. From starting out as the earth's largest book store, it has gone on to extend the brand into selling CDs, videos, DVDs, toys and games, and now auctioneering. The recently introduced 'Delight-O-Meter', which tracks Amazon.com sales, recorded 2.5 million items ordered in the first week of its operation.

Amazon's success is a combination of great choice, good value and one of the best online shopping experiences. It has also managed to support this with after-sales service and operational processes that have created trust and assurance in the brand. The organization was one of the first dot.coms to realize that maximizing market share and creating customer loyalty were key to online success. However, unlike many dot.coms, there are encouraging signs that the organization is beginning to translate its huge revenues and repeat business into bottom line results.

19

Jeff Bezos
Chief Executive Officer

Brands can stand for concrete things or abstract things. I like abstract brands because they're more flexible. Our brand stands for something very abstract because we start with the customer and work backwards. Because of this, we know we can't do something that doesn't have at least some significant twist or innovation that improves the customer experience. I'm asked all the time, 'When are you guys going to open physical stores, because Amazon is such a great brand?' Our brand would leverage into the physical world, and we could have a wonderful set of stores. There is a pragmatic reason though, from a branding point of view, why it would be difficult for us to do this. If we just opened a chain of physical stores and it looked just like someone else's chain, our customers would say, 'Well what's the big deal? I expected a little bit more. I expected you guys to do something interesting and unique', and there goes a piece of your brand value. That's the way in which your brand limits you, just as your reputation limits you. For example, if you have a reputation as a Hollywood bad boy, well then, you have to be bad occasionally. You know you can't be seen as being good all the time. That's because your brand is limiting you. It's your reputation.

The reputation of a person is such a good analogy. Somebody's reputation is largely based on what they actually do as opposed to what they actually say. That's like a brand. It has always seemed to me that your brand is formed primarily, not by what your company says about itself, but by what the company does. Some of the attributes of our brand are that people think of Amazon as a very reliable and innovative company. People associate innovation with the Amazon brand because we've been very innovative. The reason that people associate reliability with the brand – and this is almost too simple to state – is because we've worked incredibly hard to meet customer promises. If you want to have a brand that stands for reliability, then you'd better be reliable. You can have the world's best advertising campaign saying that you are reliable, but unless you are, I don't think it will do any good.

Our mission is to be earth's most customer-centric company. For us, being customer-centric means three things: listen, invent, and personalize. Listen is the most traditional form of customer centricity. Invent is there because in a highly evolving industry, if you only listen to customers you cannot succeed because you need to invent on their behalf. It's not their job to invent. They have their own businesses, they have their own lives, so we need to invent for them in our realm. The third is personalization, putting each customer in the centre of his or her universe. That's what it means for us to be customer-centric. It is our mission because we want to raise the worldwide bar for customer experience. Customer experience is bigger than customer service in that it is the full, end-to-end experience. It starts when you first hear about Amazon from a friend, and it ends when you get the package in the mail and open it.

I think our company got this culture of customer obsession through pure luck, because when we began in July of 1995 we were woefully unprepared. In the original business plan we thought it would take years and years before we had any substantial level of sales. That turned out not to be the case and in the first 30 days we took orders from all 50 states and 45 different countries. At that time there were only about 10 people in the company, and everybody had to drop everything they were doing. It didn't matter whether they were working on the software or whatever their job was. Everybody in the company basically stopped doing whatever they were doing and started working on servicing customers. If you were working on the software, for example, you would work on it for maybe six hours in the morning, and then go to the distribution centre and work until two in the morning. When your hands are that close to the customer, you get a very visceral feel for how important that customer experience is. So, early in our history we had the great good fortune of having every single person, without exception, directly servicing customers. We had an 800 number and no matter what your 'day job' was, what you really did for the first few months was to take phone calls from customers.

Everybody in the company ended up having an almost paternalistic feeling for this customer experience. Then that feeling just grew. One of the things that you find in companies is that once a culture is formed, it takes nuclear weaponry to change it. It can be great or it can be bad, depending on whether the culture fits the mission of the company.

The good news is that by the time we had 100 people in the company, all 100 of those people were stretching like crazy to make sure we had a great customer experience. If you're person number 101 and if it's not your cup of tea to stretch and go the extra mile to make sure our customer experience is great, you're going to have an allergic reaction to the company. You probably won't stay. If you do try to stay, but can't adapt to the culture then it rejects you like a virus from a healthy immune system. You either leave on your own because it's not the right place for you, or the culture rejects you.

In May of '97 we were known for six months or so as 'Amazon.toast' because that was when the bigger companies started coming online, and some very smart people were worried that they would steamroll us. The press quoted very knowledgeable people saying, 'They've had a great two-year run but it's over'. So I brought our people together in a meeting and said, 'I want you to be afraid. In fact, you should wake up terrified every morning with your sheets drenched in sweat. But don't be afraid of our competitors, be afraid of our customers, because those are the folks with whom we have a relationship'. The culture is self-reinforcing because you have a group of 250 people who put the customer first, and that's also the way that you pull together in times of adversity. You can't have 8,000 people in the company and have a group of only 25 who are the customer-experience team. That doesn't work. The only way that I know of to have good customer experience is to have a culture of good customer experience. You focus on the thing that's shared. It's worked extremely well for us.

It's the job of every person in this company to reinforce the culture, including me, so I'm a broken record on the customer experience. I've spent a lot of time over the last 18 months making sure people understand, as we focus more and more on operating efficiency, that there is no tradeoff

19

Good process frees you from the tyranny of doing the same thing over and over and reinventing it each time

on the customer experience. People sometimes believe that there must be a tradeoff but it's not the case. When you work on defect reduction and reducing variation, you find that you save a ton of money and the customer experience gets better. It's a win win. One of the things that you have to be constantly on guard against is 'either/or' thinking because although there are sometimes tradeoffs, if you apply enough problem-solving skills you can often get both.

One of the most significant costs in any business is acquiring and retaining customers. What brands do in a quantitative way is reduce the cost of customer acquisition and customer retention. Brands are very important financially for companies because they reduce those costs so much.

In our first year of operation we didn't have a dollar of paid advertising. One hundred percent of our growth came from word of mouth, and that's because we didn't have enough capital to do any paid advertising. Even today, when we spend a significant amount of money on paid advertising, a vast majority of our customers come to us by word of mouth. If you make a customer unhappy in the physical world, they might tell five friends. If you make someone unhappy online, they might tell 5,000 people through Usenet news groups, list-serves and email. The internet is an excellent many-to-many communications platform so it really does give every customer the ability to buy ink by the barrel. Likewise if you make a customer really happy and he or she turns into an evangelist, he or she can also tell thousands of potential customers. I think the internet has been an accelerant for word of mouth. I think that's true for all businesses, not just online businesses.

Everything starts with your people. Then you need good process, which is very important in any company. People misunderstand that because as soon as they hear the word 'process' they think 'bureaucracy', but bureaucracy is bad process. Good process frees you from the tyranny of doing the same thing over and over and reinventing it each time. Repetition is just downright dull. Good process eliminates unnecessary repetition. No matter what size the company is, there should be a process for anything that happens over and over. It's silly not to.

Because of the way the company grew up, we're blessed at all levels with an incredibly diverse and creative group of people who need to innovate. It's because all the early people we attracted to Amazon came here because they really wanted to be part of a pioneering company. So you attract a bunch of pioneers and then that self-reinforces because they want to do something different. We have great people partly because we had a good process for hiring in the early days. We had reference checking and a whole bunch of things that had to be done in the formal way of having hiring meetings at which we made decisions on particular candidates. There is such a diversity of people it seems as though we were selecting for just a couple of dimensions. You had to be customer obsessed and you had to want to be part of a pioneering company. You had to want to work 60-plus hours a week. No one who wanted to work 40 hours a week was going to be happy here. It was impossible. It's still impossible. That's not a value judgement. There's nothing wrong with working 40 hours a week, and there are a lot of great companies that are organized that way. It just doesn't work here. We're doing too much and we're moving too fast. In a way, by having just a few key things that you insist on leads to more diversity because you end up not caring at all about the other characteristics.

In the early days we made sure that we never allowed ourselves the luxury of lowering the bar, even during hyper growth and we've raised the bar every year since. During every year's holiday season we've done a better job than in the previous year. We measure that very carefully. It's gotten harder every year, but we've been more and more prepared every year. We've had a more experienced team of people working on it each year, and, as the scale of the holiday season gets bigger, we raise the bar on how we want to deliver against that challenge.

What we're able to offer is always changing because of advances in technology. For two decades now the price/performance ratio in microprocessors has doubled roughly every 18 months. Currently the cost of disk space is halving every 12 months and bandwidth is getting twice as cheap every nine months. That means five years from now we will be able to use 60 times as much bandwidth per customer as we do today which gives us all kinds of options. The technology alone does nothing. It's the innovation that you layer on top of the technology that becomes meaningful to the customer. Technology gets so much more powerful so quickly that, as long as you have a culture of innovation, you wake up every day thinking of what you can do for customers.

You have to understand that we have been incredibly lucky. Even some of the decisions we made in the early days that were bad calls turned out by luck to have been the right decision. We are a company that went from zero to $3 billion in sales in six years so they had to have been incredibly lucky decisions. I'll give you an example. When we were just getting started, we were advised by anybody who knew anything that we should not launch with a million titles, because a huge physical bookstore only carries about 150,000 titles and there are few that are that large. The reasonable advice was to start with 300,000, because you're going to have a devil of a time sourcing the bottom 700,000. We really had our hearts set on the million and we thought about it a lot and we decided let's just go for it. It turned out the people who advised us against the million were correct. Sourcing the bottom 700,000 almost killed us, but we did it just through sheer force of will. It actually turned out to be the thing we were best known for in our first few months. The word of mouth that accelerated the company in the early days was focused on the fact that people said, 'Hey, I'd been looking for this book for three years and I ordered it from this company and a few weeks later I had it'. By any objective standard it was a bad decision that worked out really well. There are some investment decisions that we would change if we could start over again, but we put such a priority on the customer experience that I don't think there's anything we would do differently.

19

Jeff Wilke
Senior Vice-President, Operations

I have an incredible bias that you cannot build a brand in the long run without having efficient operations. I think in the short term, good marketers and advertisers can sell water as gold. However, in the long run, the thing that's going to matter is availability, purity, taste, and, can you deliver. The problem is that the infrastructure to deliver any brand promise to a customer takes more time than it takes to build the promise. It can destroy the value of the brand faster than anything else can.

Jeff decided that building capability in operations and fulfilment was fundamentally important to the customer experience. He says this all the time, as do I, that in the long run, we may not have to own all of the assets that ship our product, but you can be certain we're going to have to have the capability and know-how to manage and audit them. When asking someone else to partner with us, they had better be able to deliver the same experience we deliver ourselves, or they are not going to be working with us for long.

The largest-sized organization where you can directly touch the minds of the folks is about 800 or so. That means the founder touches the people who work for him or her directly and they touch everybody else. Once you get above 800 or 1,000, you're serving another layer. The risk is that the mental model of the founder, which is customer-centric in this case, becomes diluted by a confused layer that has been recently hired and wasn't a part of the initial growth or initial dogma. The way to get around that risk is to have superb leadership, to audit weekly and to have many conversations with people so that you understand their mental model. You're not just pitching PowerPoint slides. You understand the decisions that they make and you model those decisions. If I'm talking about the customer experience but do a business review at a fulfilment centre and the only thing that I talk about is their cost, they're eventually going to shift all of their attention to cost and less to the customer experience. My problem with leadership training is that in many organizations, by the time the PowerPoint presentation is given beyond two or three levels, people are just reading slides.

I'm a process-oriented person; you have to have processes that are consistent with the mental model. So, process comes first; then measurement and accountability. If you focus on processes, you'll get whatever you measure and you'll get bad processes developing as a result. You have to do those two together, and you have to have exceptional leadership. Those are the three points of the triangle. The easiest thing for a company that worries about dollars is to cut costs by firing people, closing plants, cutting corners. The hard thing to do is to review the complete package and keep the balance between revenue, cost and the customer experience, to build the brand.

David Risher

Senior Vice-President, Marketing Merchandising

The Amazon brand pillars are, first, a very, very broad selection and secondly, great prices. We are fundamentally a fixed-cost model and can drive volume over a fixed-cost base and offer lower prices to the customers. We have great service, and great service, of course, means something different from what it means in the physical world in some ways. It means that not only do we make promises, but also every time we say we are going to get something for you, we get it to you on time. It means that if you have a question, or if you have a problem, we respond to you in under six hours or whatever, but it also means that we can comb through our 20 million item inventory and recommend exactly the right one to you.

In November and December 100 percent of the management and marketing boards spend at least five days, most spend closer to two weeks, at the distribution centres. It's not optional. Should I say, it's not optional for the senior leaders because it's not optional for the junior people in the company. You can't very well expect people to mess around with their Christmas time unless you are willing to do the same. It is critically important for us economically, frankly. It helps us do some load balancing; it's many extra hands to move boxes around. In addition, it helps answer the question of will this company be as focused on customers five years from now?

This company only exists because we put customers first. The University of Michigan customer satisfaction index gave us a score of 84. If you compare us to Southwest Airlines or Nordstrom or Costco or any other guys that have good service reputations, we compare favourably to them. Thirty-three million people have purchased from us, and in the last 12 months about 20 million people have repurchased. We have about 20 million active customers. Right now, something like 74, 75 percent of our business comes from repeat customers.

I look at our brand and I compare it to a brand like Virgin, or even a brand like Disney, both of which are, first of all, very customer-focused brands, and both of which are applied to a broad range of products and services. In Virgin's case, it's from a cola to an airline to cell phone service. It doesn't mean that every one of them is successful, by the way; some of those brand applications have been more successful than others. But every one of them has, in the case of Virgin, a certain innovative, customer-first and anti-traditional aspect to it.

I don't see how a company that believes that it wants to provide exceptional – not just good but exceptional – service to its customers, can ever be in a position where the external facing guys and the internal facing guys aren't always checking on each other. There may be examples of it in history, but I would be very surprised to find that in a long-term sustainable way, you have great customer companies where the marketing team is not somehow intimately involved with the development of the product and service. And vice versa – where the product and service doesn't fundamentally colour what you're saying to the outside world. It's all well and good in business school to say great customer service matters. But at the end of the day, you have to accept that at such a deep level, you almost never even question it.

Maryam Mohit

Vice-President, Site Development

When I interviewed at Amazon, there were 20 people in the company and a couple of months later there were 60 people. Most people didn't know what the internet was, and even people who knew what the internet was didn't know you could buy stuff over it. We had to earn every single person's trust through that experience. Jeff really had a very strong philosophy of underpromise and overdeliver. Don't say you're going to do 10 if you're only going to do five. If you think you're going to do five, say you're going to do three. Really try to earn that trust and surprise people in positive ways.

An early example of this was when authors would come through our offices to speak with us and maybe do an interview with us. We asked them to autograph a bunch of books, and we thought maybe we would sell these signed copies as a different category as they do in bookstores. Instead we decided not to distinguish between books that were autographed and those that were not. We just wrote a little letter on Amazon letterhead and slipped it into those copies. It said, 'We have this autographed copy and we sent it to you because we thought you might enjoy it'.

Sometimes I talk with friends who work at other companies and they say, 'I'm in the marketing department and nobody cares about the customers and that's frustrating. Why is it that at Amazon it seems as though everyone cares?' It makes me think that it's a leadership thing. I ask my friends, 'What does your CEO think about that? Doesn't he or she say that this is important?' They say, 'They're focused on other issues'. Jeff is very strong on customer centricity. The people who are successful at Amazon are also strong in customer centricity, so it self-reinforces.

We do a ton of listening to customers. I take it for granted, but I've heard people at other companies say that it's not common practice. We read customer emails and we do user tests every week; we also do focus groups and we do facility testing. We get tons of information from customer service when people write to us, but it's really important to know how to use that information and not just take it at face value. It's necessary to interpret the customers, not just take them word for word.

Without good design and good technology in the website, you don't have a store. Without good operations and fulfilment and without a system for customer service, you don't sell. You need all of these different elements, and you need vendor relations. I think interrelatedness in our business is a fact. That's the way it is. If we say on the website that a product usually ships in 24 hours, the order has to go through software that tells the warehouse what to do. Then customer service has to know about it and it has to show up on the website in the customer's account area when the customer checks on their order. It also has to generate an email to the customer. It is so interrelated that it seems like a global ecosystem. That is the biology of our corporation; interrelated and interdisciplinary.

Conclusion

What did we learn?

When we set out to write this book we wanted to find out what makes our chosen brands unique – how they managed to create enthusiastic customers and levels of employee loyalty that competitors dream of. Our premise that these companies have cultures uniquely developed to meet the needs of their customers in a distinctive way was certainly validated, however, whilst each of these companies is very different, there are also some striking similarities in the way they operate. These characteristics, whilst shared with each other, are still 'uncommon practice' as far as the majority of organizations are concerned and help to explain why these brands are so powerful. This final chapter summarizes these 'uncommon practices' and gives examples of how they are brought to life in the organizations we studied.

Their leaders are profoundly customer-centric

Being customer-centred is hardly a new idea. There is probably not a large organization today that does not feature customer service as a core value. Read their annual report and customer service will often be mentioned as a key performance indicator. However, the difference between the way most executives talk about customers and how the uncommon practice leaders do is very different. It is not one of the things that they pay attention to, it is the main thing they pay attention to. It is the way that they lead their business lives every day. Concepts like the 'Balanced Business Scorecard' (Kaplan and Norton) have been helpful in introducing the notion that the bottom line is just one of the metrics that a company must focus on. However, it does not go far enough; it implies that there is a tradeoff to be struck between doing what is right for customers and the costs of doing so.

The leaders we spoke to operate from a profound sense of what they believe is right for customers. They are passionate about customer service to the extent of making, what would seem to most organizations, irrational decisions. For example, in the case of Carphone Warehouse, offering a free repair service to people who had not purchased their phone from the company. These decisions are not taken on the basis that they are the best way to optimize profits; they are taken because they are the right things to do for customers. In the words of Charles Dunstone: 'We basically have a very childlike dream really, we absolutely fervently believe that if you have to buy a mobile phone, there is nowhere better, no organization that will care more about you than we do'.

That raises another issue about customer centricity: the leaders of these organizations take personal responsibility for walking the talk and creating cultures that support the strategy. Amazon.com's Jeff Bezos was very clear with us that 'Our mission is to be the earth's most customer-centred company'. Many organizations have mission statements that say similar things but few have leaders who take personal responsibility for holding the organization true to them. According to Jeff Bezos: 'It's the job of every person in this company to reinforce the culture, including me, so I'm a broken record on the customer experience. I've spent a lot of time over the last 18 months making sure people understand, as we focus more and more on operating efficiency, that there is no tradeoff on the customer experience'.

This raises another important principle and that is that this customer centricity is integral to the way the company is run. These leaders do not talk about customer focus as though it is a nice value to have but only loosely connected to the strategy or brand; they see them as one and the same. Finally, these leaders are clear about what is important and they live it. Uncommon practice leaders 'walk the talk'; they do not 'stumble the mumble'.

The customer experience, the brand and the strategy are inseparable

We typically began our interviews by asking the executives to define their brands. In many cases they started by talking about the customer experience that they set out to create; the brand was almost an afterthought. Common practice has it that you define your brand and then communicate this to the marketplace through advertising and promotion and then you deliver it to customers. More recently organizations have begun to realize that they should also 'live the brand' and have engaged companies like Forum and Interbrand to turn the brand values into front-line brand behaviours. Many (although not all) companies featured in this book have taken a different approach starting with the product or customer experience and letting that determine the brand.

This flow through of the customer experience to the brand is very much evident at easyGroup. Stelios Haji-Ioannou founded easyJet by identifying an unmet market need for a low-cost airline in Europe. He realized that in order to create assurance for customers, the airline had to have the latest aircraft and high standards of operational efficiency, so the only way to achieve the lower costs that the strategy demanded was by cutting out the sales intermediaries and travel agents and having a direct channel to the market. That, in turn, demanded a brand that customers notice. To quote Stelios: 'The need to communicate directly to our customers created another need in the company and that is to be high profile, brash and "in your face" because you can't be quiet and reticent and expect customers to find your phone number and look for you'.

In the immediate aftermath of the terrorist attacks on the World Trade Centre, the airline industry virtually collapsed, with major airlines laying off staff and seeking governmental support. easyJet bucked the trend, enjoying full aircraft and strong demand. This close integration of customer experience, brand and strategy introduces another fundamental principle.

Companies must simultaneously excel at customer intimacy, operational excellence and product leadership

One school of thought has it that you must choose to differentiate by being superior at customer intimacy, product leadership or operational excellence. What we found was that many of these companies, whilst having a dominant focus, seem to be competitively strong in their people, products and operational processes all at the same time. Phil Satre of Harrah's put this into perspective by saying: 'Our core strategy is customer intimacy – focusing on the customer [... we cannot] ignore product [... we cannot] ignore cost efficiencies [...] The market won't let us. Our customers won't let us'.

This integration of service, process and product is fundamental to the strategy of Amazon.com. Its business model is based on having an extensive product range, efficient processes and keen pricing and very customer-focused people. Maryam Mohit told us: 'Without good design and good technology in the website, you don't have a store. Without good operations and fulfilment and without a system for customer service, you don't sell. You need all of these different elements, and you need vendor relations. I think interrelatedness [...] is a fact. That's the way it is'.

It is almost as if in daring to be different these brands are passionate about everything that they do. This is evident in Pret A Manger's culture. CEO Andrew Rolfe emphasized: 'We're not concerned about having consistency of brand so much as about consistency of purpose that flows throughout the whole of the organization. It doesn't actually matter what we write on the napkins or say through advertising, all that matters is that when you go into a Pret shop you get that set of experiences that describes Pret. The way that you interact with our team members in our shop, the way our suppliers interact with us, the way we develop new products and services. That's Pret. Just being very, very passionate about the things we care about'.

This ability to simultaneously focus on customer service, product development and operational processes creates a natural synergy that is self-reinforcing and creates a customer offer that is almost impossible to beat. A great example of this is First Direct which single-handedly redefined the retail banking industry in the UK. The organization has incredible customer loyalty and acquires a new customer every four seconds through direct referral. This has been achieved by creating totally new operational processes to support its strategy of 24-hour banking, new products to meet the needs of its highly targeted customers and customer service that is legendary. When First Direct started out, its executives identified that in order for its strategy to be successful, it had to adopt our next uncommon practice.

The customer experience and the employee experience are inextricably linked

This theme seems so self-evident that to state it seems almost unnecessary, yet how many companies intentionally set out to create a culture that is designed to complement the customer experience? The people at Midland Bank were so aware of this that they realized that they needed to create not only a new brand called First Direct to communicate the proposition but also a totally separate company and culture to deliver it. This alignment of the employee experience with the customer experience was a conscious decision at First Direct: 'We ensure that our internal brand values are the same as our external ones. It seems to me that there must be a mirror between the two. You can't pretend to be one style of brand to your consumers if you're a different style of brand to your people'.

Julian Richer of Richer Sounds makes this link between the customer experience and the employee experience even more explicit and takes a very uncommon approach to creating a distinctive employment experience for his best performing 'colleagues' by providing Bentleys for the weekend, trips on the company jet and holiday homes. Common sense would say that this is a very expensive way of rewarding people and most organizations would opt for the more conventional 'Employee of the Month' award.

Julian Richer has a very different view and one that explains why his shops are in the record books for the highest number of sales per square foot in the world: 'My definition of culture is your perception of the organization as an employee. So for the culture to be a good, positive, happy one, employees have to believe in it, and that will only come through lots of effort. At the end of the day, the Bentleys cost very little, the jet is flying anyway, the holiday homes we provide cost a few thousand a year but the downside cost of having disgruntled or demotivated employees is phenomenal. It's absenteeism, labour turnover, theft, bad customer service. So I would argue that what I spend on these things is worth every penny'.

Lest you think that Julian Richer is a 'soft touch' when it comes to employee welfare, Richer Sounds is one of the tightest run retail operations that you will find anywhere. He is proud of the fact that he is as quick to demote people as he is to promote them. Rather, what it shows is that it is possible to be employee focused as well as have very tight financial controls. Uncommon practice is about managing dilemmas so that business moves from a mindset of either/or to and/both. This mirroring of the employee and customer experiences requires human resource departments to become much more strategic in their development of HR practices to support the business.

Human resource practices support the customer experience

We find it amazing how many organizations talk about offering the most friendly call centre employees, or having the best trained financial advisors, but have HR policies that are essentially the same as everyone else's. Uncommon practice requires that different strategies require different capabilities; different capabilities require different attitudes and skills, and these, in turn, come from different hiring, training and reward practices.

David Mead at First Direct makes this link between HR practices and the customer experience: 'We passionately believe that every customer is an individual and requires unique and personalized service. To make sure that our people genuinely believe that and believe that principle on each and every occasion, we also focus very strongly on the individual within First Direct'.

The organization 'walks the talk' by offering employees a package of benefits that enables the individual to tailor their particular remuneration to their stage in life. David goes on to say: 'In order to reinforce the primary importance of individuality with the customer, we seek to do the same with our people, so we talk about individual people here in the same way as we talk about individual customers externally'.

The key is to know the key levers to press to support your strategy rather than being average in all things. Chris Stone VP of Human Resources for Midwest Express makes this very point; 'From our people's standpoint, what do we have to do especially well? Do you have to do performance management pretty well? Yes, you have to do it, but it doesn't have to be "state of the art". What about pay and benefits? No, you don't have to do that incredibly well. You do have to meet people's needs and you do have to have some flexibility [...]. But more than anything, what you have to do really well in a customer-intimate environment is to hire the right people'.

This means that the people with the best business qualifications may not be the best people for the job; an understanding of what makes a great customer moment is more important than an understanding of how to benchmark trends in a marketplace. In one sense it's important to forget about whether someone has the right MBA and to think about whether they have the right DNA. All of the principles described so far create a foundation for delivering a customer experience that is so intentional, consistent, different and valuable to the target customers that it becomes synonymous with the brand: what we call a 'Branded Customer Experience'.

Deliver a branded customer experience

A perfect example of this is Harley-Davidson. John Russell, the CEO of Harley-Davidson Europe told us, '[...] we started out with a great product that, in our case, was a motorcycle. The founders of the company didn't sit there with a brand plan in that shed in Wisconsin in 1903; they decided they wanted to design a motorcycle. That motorcycle took on certain characteristics which then determined the product experience: how the motorcycle feels, how it looks, what it sounds like. So all of those things begin to evolve into a product-related experience for the customer'.

But the Harley brand is so much more than the bike itself. The organization has intentionally created a range of other services to differentiate the brand and create value for customers. John talks about this as 'going to the edge of the brand experience'. '[…] it's all about exploring the potential for developing the experience. The things that are seen as leading edge and totally innovative become the bread and butter of our brand experience. We're developing riding experiences through rentals in holiday locations, Harley world tours, where we take you on an organized tour of self-discovery. Our job is to keep adding to these experiences. What drives us to do that is our customers'. When you have a brand as valuable as Harley-Davidson, you sustain it and develop it even if that is sometimes at the expense of maximizing short-term profit.

The branded customer experience should not be compromised in the interest of short-term profit

It is easy to talk about putting principles before profit but harder to do when faced with the numbers. Carphone Warehouse refunding £10 million to customers, because the price of their mobile phone had fallen after they had purchased it, is a rare example of putting the principles of the company ahead of the bottom line, although interestingly, Charles Dunstone went on to say that the company had been even more profitable since implementing that policy.

One of the most common growth strategies for companies is to acquire others or merge. It is also one of the quickest ways to erode shareholder value if the intended synergies fail to materialize. In the rush towards consolidation it takes a clear head to remember the core values of the brand and stay true to them even though the opportunity is a profitable one. Phil Satre of Harrah's recalled one such opportunity: 'I remember considering a decision – 12 years ago – to acquire a company in the lottery industry. It was a very attractive opportunity. But we said, "Where does that fit with our values? There's no relationship with the customer. We don't know who they are. 'Yes, it's the gambling industry, but it isn't what we stand for'. As a result, Harrah's declined that opportunity even though it was very attractive financially and would have made money for the organization.

This is not to say that these organizations are any less commercially aware than the norm. Far from it. We found that they had a very clear focus on their operation and results. Rather, they do not see profit as the primary reason that the organization exists.

Sustaining the customer experience over time depends on really understanding what your customers expect and value and measuring this constantly. This knowledge comes from listening to customers, and measuring the customer experience in a variety of ways, as opposed to the more common customer-questionnaire approach that so many organizations take. Krispy Kreme uses digital cameras to record the customer experience so that managers can see the actual problem, not just read about it.

Companies zealously acquire and use customer knowledge

Measuring customer satisfaction is the norm, measuring the customer experience is not. Krispy Kreme captures data from a number of sources: 'Instead of a customer-service department, [words are important and what things are called is very important] we developed and implemented a customer-experience group. Instead of looking at quantitative sales measures, we established measures through mystery shoppers and our own internal inspections as well as solicitation of off-premises customers through internal surveys. We are receiving information all the time. We try to bring it to a level where we have a great deal of confidence in the information'.

Understanding their customers has become a key differentiator for RBC Financial Group. The organization initially introduced a customer-relationship management system to be more targeted in their promotional activity but are increasingly using the system to acquire knowledge of customers to enhance the service the bank provides. Judith Hatley, VP, Marketing and Customer Management told us: 'We are building something called customer preference and choice'. It is interesting nobody else has done it yet. 'We are building capability ... [so that we can find out personal information from you that you want us to know]. For example, "don't ever call me up after seven o'clock in the evening", or, "please call me at work"'. This is moving the bank from customer-relationship management to customer-managed relationships, placing the control in the hands of customers to determine how and when they wished to be served.

What about those myths?

In our introduction we mentioned that there were various preconceptions about running businesses that we wanted to explore. Here are the answers that we think emerge from this book.

Should you assume that the customer is always right?

Not always. Most organizations serve customers that are unprofitable or do not fit the business model. easyGroup is very clear that its business model will not be attractive to 50 percent of the population and that is fine by them. The right customer is always right would be more accurate. Moreover, particularly when you are developing a new idea for customers, it is often impossible for a customer to have a meaningful opinion. 'They don't know what they don't know'.

Who should come first, your people or your customers?

A total commitment to your customer must be at the heart of your business but it is your people you need to consider first. Your people have to put the customer first. If you have hired the right people, and trained and developed them well, then they will take care of the customer.

Is a focus on the bottom line the main driver of financial success?

Not necessarily. In the words of Sir Stuart Hampson, it is better to 'focus on the drivers of profit rather than the profit itself'. This means paying attention to other measures, particularly measures of customer satisfaction, brand equity, staff satisfaction rather than just sales figures.

Are external communications more important than internal communications?

They are equally important. Great brand building starts from the inside out. Imaginative, well-executed communications that segment internal audiences in the same way that you would segment external audiences are vital.

Is harmonizing the culture the first step following a merger?

No, harmonizing two distinct cultures can lead to a dilution of both. The important thing is to establish as quickly as possible the culture that best supports the desired customer experience and make this dominant. When Carphone Warehouse acquired Tandy it sent out the strongest signal as to what kind of culture it would be building by sending directors up to a Tandy warehouse in Birmingham to sort out distribution problems.

Which is more important: hiring right or training right?

Both of these are important but clearly the most important is to 'hire right'. Hire for attitude is the mantra of all our companies, because skills can be learnt. But training right is important – and by training right we mean training that reinforces the distinct culture you wish to build and enables people to deliver the brand. That often means designing specific modules and equipping your own people to train their colleagues. Avoid hiring in contract trainers if they are going to give you the same kind of programmes that everyone else in the marketplace has.

Is advertising and promotion the fastest way to build a brand?

Probably not – the fastest way to build a brand is through 'word of mouth marketing, high-profile PR and bold and imaginative product or service offers that command attention'. Advertising can be important in maintaining and developing the brand – but almost all of these companies either don't advertise at all (Pret A Manger), advertise conservatively (John Lewis) or first established themselves as brands in the minds of a group of loyal customers before they advertised heavily (eg Virgin, Amazon).

Is investing in the 'soft stuff' a waste of time?

No. No. A thousand times no. Investing in 'soft stuff' produces 'hard results' whether in improved employee productivity, higher retention levels or greater customer satisfaction, all of which are drivers of profitability.

Is it true that you should hire the best MBAs you can find?

Again, not necessarily. Many – if not most – of the leaders of the companies in this book do not have a classic MBA training, in fact they might not have achieved as much if they had followed many classic management rules. They are much more concerned with 'fit' than 'smarts'; more 'EQ' than 'IQ'. This does not mean that you should ignore MBAs – the vast majority of whom are extremely talented – but an MBA on its own is not enough. As we have said before, attitude is the most important attribute – so 'think less about MBA and more about DNA!'

Is 'walking the talk' an overused cliché?

Yes, it is overused but underutilized in that it is often said but rarely put into practice. The people in this book use the phrase a lot (in fact, we were surprised at how often we heard it) but they mean it and they live by it as a creed, not as a trite management mantra.

To sum up

These principles although common sense are uncommon practice. Whilst many organizations may exhibit some of them, the brands that we studied live most of them. It is this holistic view of the organization and brand that makes these organizations the winners that they are. As we said before, we did not set out to identify a 'quick fix' for organizations wishing to strengthen their brand since we know that it is the application of these principles that drives business success, not the awareness of them. They are still uncommon practice because it is the former that is exceptionally difficult to do. Some of these principles will not come as any great surprise to experienced branding practitioners; nevertheless, we have summed them up for the benefit of all our readers, as shown on the opposite page.

Uncommon Practices

Customer-centric leadership

Ownership of the customer experience at board level

Leaders who walk the talk

Leaders spend significant time with customers and employees

Avoidance of bureaucracy – no back office

Distinctive strategy/proposition

Founder's vision permeates the company

Customer need determines the strategy

Clear customer proposition

Integrated strategy – the customer experience, the strategy and the brand are inseparable

Superior products, processes and people

Innovative processes

Distinctive products

Supportive technology

Superior customer skills and capabilities

Internal culture that supports the strategy

Internal values aligned with brand values

Endemic and enduring 'DNA'

Passionate people

Employee experience mirrors the customer experience

Aligned HR systems

HR strategy, systems and training support the customer experience

Recruitment for attitude and fit (DNA)

Innovative reward systems

Clear consequences for good/bad performance

Branded customer experience

Customer experience – intentional, consistent, differentiated and valuable

Obsession with protecting and managing the brand

Whole company focus on the customer experience

Strong alignment between marketing, operations and HR around the brand

Experience measurement

Clear focus on target customers

Measurement of the experience not just satisfaction

Rapid feedback to the front line

Focus on sources of profit not just the bottom line

About the Editors

Andy Milligan is the Director of Interbrand's Internal Brand Management practice. He has run brand consulting projects internationally dealing with issues such as brand positioning, brand portfolio development and corporate identity. He now advises companies on how to use their brand promise and values as a force for internal change.

Andy is a regular conference speaker and contributor of articles on branding issues as well as being one of Interbrand's principal media spokespeople.

His work has included projects for a diverse range of organizations such as Jacuzzi Corp, Standard Life, ATP, Barclays, BiC, London Underground, FIFA, Roche Diagnostics and Cussons.

Shaun Smith is Senior Vice-President of Forum's Customer Experience Business. He is responsible for directing client projects that address a wide range of business issues including: building executive alignment, implementing customer-focused change and helping companies define and deliver customer experiences that differentiate their brands.

Shaun speaks to audiences in a variety of industries on the subjects of customer focus and brand delivery. He has appeared several times on CNBC's 'Ask the Expert' programme and is registered with Speakers for Business and the London Speakers Bureau. Shaun has published a number of articles as well as surveys dealing with organizational alignment and customer loyalty. His next book, *Branding the Customer Experience*, is due in mid-2002.

Clients include: Microsoft, Westin Hotels, Jardine Flemings, Sainsbury's, Toyota, Disney Corporation, British Airways, The Royal Festival Hall, Cathay Pacific Airways, Leo Burnett, Shangri-La Hotels and Resorts, and many more.